5

CHARLIE CHAPLIN

A CENTENARY CELEBRATION

edited
by
Peter Haining

W. Foulsham & Co. Ltd.
London • New York • Toronto • Cape Town • Sydney

A very rare signed photograph of the young Chaplin in Hollywood.

FOREWORD

Charles Chaplin has been the most publicised figure of the cinema. There are libraries of Chaplin books; impossible, you might say, to find a new approach. Peter Haining has found it. He has searched forgotten churchyards, read obscure publications, examined the sources of unfamiliar recollections ranging from Max Linder to Groucho Marx; especially he has collected photographs, sketches, posters and cartoons. There is the background here of a life, public and private; the celebrity, but also in the distance the young player (he was nine when he got his first job) performing on the live stage, being reviewed, looking for work. Everything is there, everything seen or heard: what emerges is a portrait through other people's eyes. The guarded and the unguarded moments – but are they unguarded? When you met Chaplin (he was very social) you saw the actor: he would act a whole scene from a film, it was his substitute for conversation; you would be dazzled. You come away from this book still dazzled – but bewildered. Was this forthcoming man, as one or two recollections suggest, ungenerous to friends or colleagues? What was he really like? The spell of genius forbids an answer. Perhaps we shall never know – until somebody who didn't admire Chaplin, didn't even like him, comes out with a reaction.

And that doesn't seem round the corner.

Dilys Powell.

DILYS POWELL, THE SUNDAY TIMES.

For
My Daughter
GEMMA
'Our Kid'

Flick the pages backwards or forwards and see Charlie walking.

W. Foulsham & Company Limited
Yeovil Road, Slough, Berkshire, SL1 4JH

ISBN 0–572–01318–3

Printed in Great Britain at The Bath Press, Avon

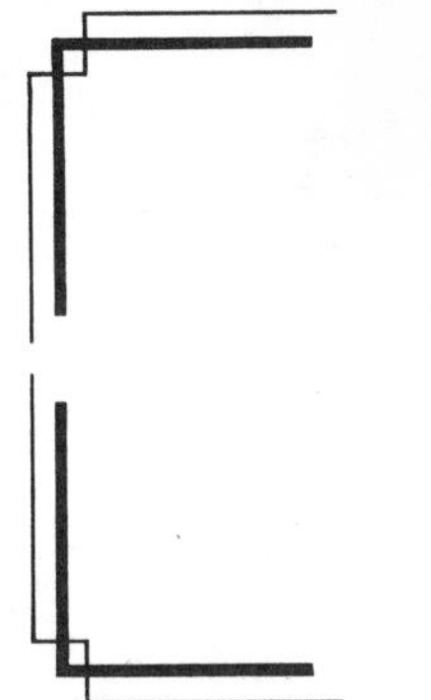

CONTENTS

The magic of Chaplin as seen by cartoonist Steve B. Drummond in *Pictures & Picturegoer*, September 18, 1915.

'There is one redeeming feature about *Jim, A Romance of Cockayne*, the part of Sammy, a newspaper boy, a smart London street Arab, much responsible for the comic part. Although hackneyed and old-fashioned, Sammy was made vastly amusing by Master Charles Chaplin, a bright and vigorous child actor. I have never heard of the boy before, but I hope to hear great things of him in the near future.'

The Topical Times
July 11, 1903

'Whatever future the cinema may have, into whatever new forms it will develop, and no matter how long it endures as a means of entertainment, Charles Chaplin is unlikely to be displaced as one of the greatest of its originals. Like British broadcasting's only great clown, Tommy Handley, Chaplin seemed made for his medium and for no other. He came to it when he and the films were both young. He perfected his genius – technique is too poor a word – with uncanny speed. He was tireless and prolific. Film after film was produced to delight millions in all countries. First the two-reelers – and some of the greatest Chaplin masterpieces are still to be found among them – later the larger efforts such as *The Gold Rush*, and *Shoulder Arms*. Finally, those commentaries on his age: *Modern Times* and *The Great Dictator*. Fortunately the film is a permanent medium; new generations need not take their parents' word where Chaplin's films are concerned. They will be able to see for themselves.'

The Times
June 27, 1962

INTRODUCTION

One hundred years ago in April 1889 three events of world significance occurred. In America, an inventor named Thomas Alva Edison created an instrument that was to revolutionise the world of entertainment, the Kinetoscope, the fore-runner of the movie camera. Three thousand miles away across the Atlantic, in Austria, a baby to be christened Adolf, was born to a minor customs official named Hitler. And in London, the wife of a moderately successful musical hall entertainer, herself a singer, produced a lusty young infant she would call Charles Spencer Chaplin.

Though unrelated at the time, these three 'births' were to be dramatically intermingled when, some years later, Charles Chaplin was to conquer the new world of entertainment that Thomas Edison had fathered and with its help ridicule the tyrant his contemporary, Adolf Hitler, had become in a film called *The Great Dictator*. It is, of course, for his undisputed mastery of comedy that Chaplin is best known, but it was through the eye of the camera that his image was to be projected to every corner of the Earth and make him, quite literally, the first man to become world famous in his own lifetime.

From his humble birth, Chaplin rose to enjoy the unique

Chaplin the supreme film-maker: two revealing photographs of Charlie at work taken half a century apart.

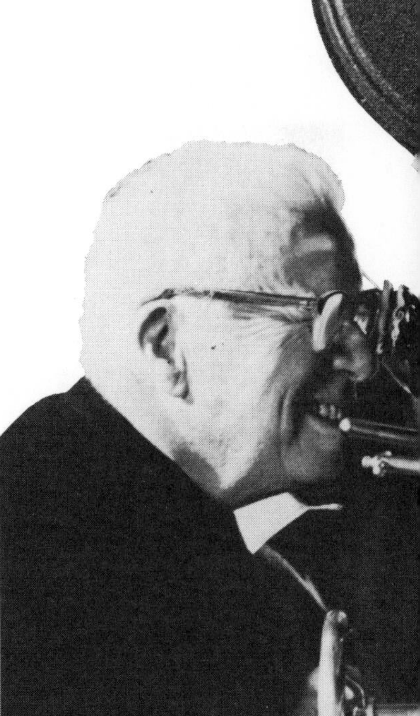

honour of having made more human beings laugh than any other actor who ever lived. And though he was later to be exiled from America, the country where he had earned his fame, because of his alleged political opinions, he was ultimately to be lauded with honours by that same nation as well as earning a knighthood in his native England. Though he ended his days as Sir Charles Chaplin, a revered figure content in his legend and living in a grand Swiss mansion, he was, and probably always will be, to his countless millions of admirers, just 'Charlie' Chaplin. That he should have died on Christmas Day, 1977, at the venerable age of 88 was perhaps only appropriate. For who other than Father Christmas has enjoyed such fame or brought such pleasure year in and year out to all the world's citizens?

Though Charlie has been the subject of a billion words, countless thousand articles, and hundreds of books, he remains something of an enigma: which is, of course, part of his fascination. Yet he himself was evidently puzzled by some elements of his achievements, and all his life was fascinated by the stories people

The world famous star visits the scenes of his childhood in London – Charlie and his wife, Oona in Kennington in 1971.

who had early-day associations with him would recall. Somehow they helped answer his unanswered questions, and as he read or listened to these stories, it would take him vividly back in his mind to long-buried incidents. Many such memories were to find their way into his fascinating though undeniably selective work, *My Autobiography*, published in 1964. But not *quite* all.

Some years ago I was intrigued to read in a London newspaper about the huge sacks of mail that Charlie invariably received whenever he returned to the city where he had been born. While he was staying at the Savoy Hotel – it was reported – his secretary would open a separate file for each of those letters which came from people who had known him in the past. Childhood friends, vaudeville colleagues, film actors and such like. A mixture of ordinary folk and the well-known. These files were always labelled with the words, 'Old Timers'.

With the passage of time, and as many of the people in a position to know about Chaplin's past died, the files were discontinued. But it intrigued me to wonder just *what* some of those letters had contained. Perhaps, I thought, some of the writers might also have written letters to the daily press about their doubtless proud associations with the star, or else talked about him in interviews they had given to the media? With this in mind, I began to comb the files of newspapers, magazines and all manner of film and entertainment journals through the years when Chaplin was alive. The result was the rich hoard of memories which now make up this book and span Chaplin's life from his childhood to old age and encompass both his private life and his career. There is a personal touch about them that somehow surpasses the more formal approach of a biography, and perhaps enables us to see the enigma that was Chaplin just a little more clearly. Their stories are augmented by some of Charlie's own previously uncollected views from the press. Plus my own research into the mysteries surrounding the little star's origins and birth as well as the surprising influences that helped make him the 'Comic genius of the cinema screen' as *The Times* headlined his Obituary.

Doubtless there will be many tributes to mark the centenary of Charlie's birth, but few, I believe, will offer quite the same intimate insights which follow. For they amount to mortals' observations of a man who had become immortal.

THE MYSTERY OF 'CHARLIE THONSTEIN' OF SUFFOLK AND LONDON

There are enough mysteries and conflicting stories about the origins, birth and early days of Charlie Chaplin to tax even the ingenuity of Sherlock Holmes (who plays a part in our history, as the reader will later discover). Investigating them is, however, both fascinating and frustrating – yet it is satisfying to have been able at least to unravel some of the most puzzling aspects of Chaplin's start in life in this the centenary year of his birth.

The mystery begins with Chaplin's very origins. To many he has always seemed the archetypal product of a Victorian Cockney background: one child among many born underfed and underprivileged in one of London's poorest districts. To these people, he appears part of a line of slum dwellers which the capital had spawned for generations. Others have believed his dark good looks point to Continental origins; that he might even have been Jewish. And a third group have seen him springing from a rural community, the off-spring of a family drawn away from the land and into the maw of London in the hope of a better life-style. In fact, there is a little truth in each of these conclusions.

During his lifetime, Charlie, like many a famous personality from undeniably humble beginnings, did little to settle the confusion over his background. At one time, he was happy to promote a rags-to-riches story of escape from the crushing poverty of London to world-wide acclaim. At another, he spoke of having French Hugenot ancestry, and of actually having been born in Fontainebleau! And on a third talked vaguely of his family roots lying in the county of Suffolk. But with the growth of his fame and an overwhelming fascination with his work, such matters seemed to decrease in importance. And with the passage of time, what evidence there *was* has become scattered if not entirely lost altogether.

The one item that might most easily have answered all the questions was Charlie's birth certificate: that normally easily accessible document lodged in Somerset House in London. But, amazingly, in the case of arguably the most famous man of the twentieth century, there is no trace of any such certificate to be found there! The law in 1889 when the infant was born was not as strict as it is now about such registration and for whatever reasons – deliberate avoidance, forgetfulness or indifference – Charlie's parents did not record his birth: though they had meticulously

done so for his older brother, Sydney, born on March 16, 1885.

There are, however, both birth and death certificates for Charlie's father, Charles Chaplin, described as a 'Comedian of Lambeth', and it is through these documents that the family's origins may be ascertained. For from the birth certificate we can learn that Charles Chaplin the father had been born on April 13, 1848 at Finborough Magnus in the County of Suffolk. Nor is this the only point of interest: for in giving his age at the time of his death

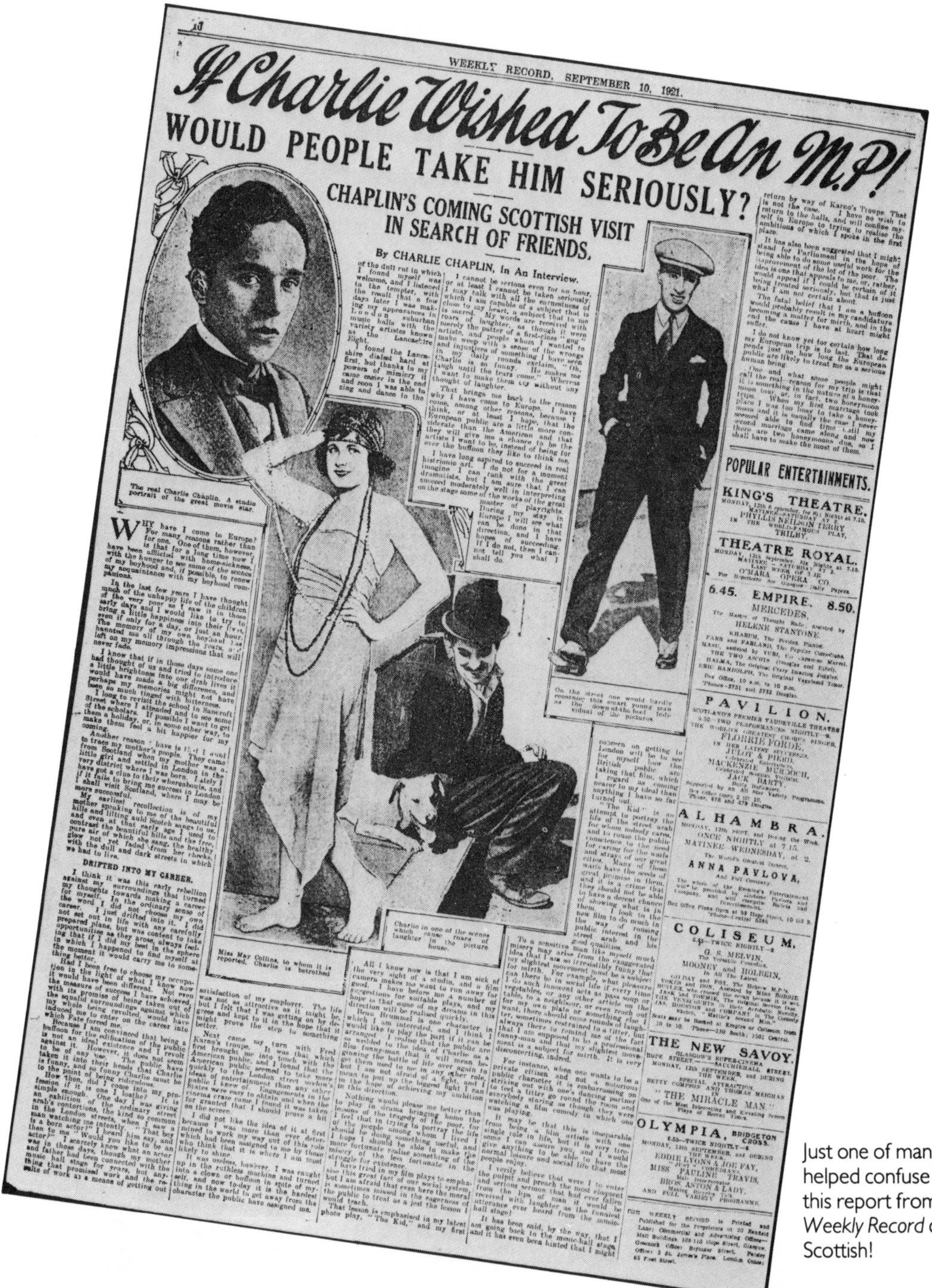

WEEKLY RECORD, SEPTEMBER 10, 1921.

If Charlie Wished To Be An M.P.!

WOULD PEOPLE TAKE HIM SERIOUSLY?

CHAPLIN'S COMING SCOTTISH VISIT IN SEARCH OF FRIENDS.

By CHARLIE CHAPLIN, In An Interview.

The real Charlie Chaplin. A studio portrait of the great movie star.

Miss May Collins, to whom it is reported, Charlie is betrothed.

Charlie in one of the scenes which cause roars of laughter in the picture house.

On the street one would hardly recognise this smart young man as the down-at-the-heel individual of the pictures.

POPULAR ENTERTAINMENTS.

Just one of many stories that have helped confuse Chaplin's origins: this report from the *Glasgow Weekly Record* claiming him to be Scottish!

CERTIFIED COPY OF AN ENTRY OF DEATH

GIVEN AT THE GENERAL REGISTER OFFICE, LONDON

Application Number R108464

REGISTRATION DISTRICT Lambeth

1901. DEATH in the Sub-district of Lambeth Church First in the County of London

Columns:—	1	2	3	4	5	6	7	8	9
No.	When and Where died	Name and surname	Sex	Age	Occupation	Cause of death	Signature, description and residence of informant	When registered	Signature of registrar
40	Ninth May 1901 St Thomas's Hospital	Charles Chaplin	Male	37 years	Comedian of Lambeth	Cirrhosis of liver Ascites Certified by [illegible] MRCS	H. Chaplin widow of deceased 16 Golden Place Chester Street Lambeth	Tenth May 1901	[illegible] Registrar

CERTIFIED to be a true copy of an entry in the certified copy of a Register of Deaths in the District above mentioned.
Given at the GENERAL REGISTER OFFICE, LONDON, under the Seal of the said Office, the 18th day of May 1988

This certificate is issued in pursuance of the Births and Deaths Registration Act 1953. Section 34 provides that any certified copy of an entry purporting to be sealed or stamped with the seal of the General Register Office shall be received as evidence of the birth or death to which it relates without any further or other proof of the entry, and no certified copy purporting to have been given in the said Office shall be of any force or effect unless it is sealed or stamped as aforesaid.

DX 411929

CAUTION:—It is an offence to falsify a certificate or to make or knowingly use a false certificate or a copy of a false certificate intending it to be accepted as genuine to the prejudice of any person, or to possess a certificate knowing it to be false without lawful authority.

GENERAL REGISTER OFFICE ENGLAND

Form A504M Dd 8098294 7640824 30M 3/88 Mcr(735708)

(Above) Death Certificate for Charlie's father which set the author on the track of the star's ancestry. (Right) The birth announcement which gives Charlie's date as April 15!

The Cradle.

On the 15th ultimo, the wife of Mr Charles Chaplin (*nee* Miss Lily Harley), of a beautiful boy. Mother and son both doing well. Papers please copy.

as '37 years' and establishing that he was born in 1848 we can see the thespian had conveniently 'lost' some 15 years of his life. No doubt a professional stratagem and obviously unknown to his wife when his death was recorded!

On the trail of Charlie's origins, reference to the Ordnance Survey map pinpoints Finborough Magnus as the modern Great Finborough, three miles to the south of the town of Stowmarket, and not that far distant from the corner of Suffolk where I have come to live. On one bright summer's day with Constable-type clouds piled high over the rolling Suffolk countryside I drove to Great Finborough, with my own great expectations. A picturesque little village straddled the B1115, with views across the green pastureland characteristic of this part of East Anglia. The spire of the local church of St Andrew's stood out above the mixture of old cottages and recently built family houses. It was to the church that I made my way.

I had expected to find myself searching for hours in the farthest corners of the churchyard for any sign of the Chaplin family but instead, close to the path leading to the front door of the church, I came across a row of tombstones of varying ages, all bearing the name Chaplin. Thanks to the research of my good friend, the reknowned genealogist, W.O.G. Lofts (who had been checking on Charlie Chaplin's forebears), I knew the names that I was looking for. Examining the stones in the warm afternoon sunlight, I sensed I had at last found the little comic's true origins.

A simple granite headstone, tilted by the years, and the surface almost obscured by litchen, proved to be that of George Chaplin, born in Finborough in 1741 and died 1819 – Charlie's great-

The row of Chaplin graves in St Andrew's Church, Great Finborough, Suffolk.

great-great-grandfather. Beside him lay his wife, Susanna, née Bacon, also of the same village, who had been born in 1749 and died in 1827.

Next, I found the grave of one of their nine children, a man with the curious name of Meshach Chaplin, who had been born in 1788, and after a lifetime farming locally had died in 1849. George and Susanna, it seemed, had a love of Old Testament names, for two of their other boys were named Shadrach and Abednego – names that stuck in my memory and came to mind later when I was looking into the stories of Charlie's supposed Jewish origins. At that moment, though, I was just interested to read the inscription on the base of the tombstone over the grave of Charlie's great-great-grandparent: 'Remember the time to serve the Lord'.

Adjacent to this plot was perhaps the most imposing of all the Chaplin graves, a small tower marking the last resting place of Daniel Chaplin, Charlie's great-grandfather, a thatcher by trade who had been born in the nearby village of Buxhall in 1802 and died in 1869. And to the left of this, the grave of Spencer Chaplin, grandfather to little Charlie, born in 1834 and died in 1897, probably without ever having seen the child destined for what would at the time have seemed unimaginable fame. According to local information, for a time this forebear ran a grocery and draper's shop at 38, High Road, leaving the village about the time the local school was built near these premises in 1881.

One last fascinating headstone remained. Rebecca Chaplin – it proclaimed at the top – died January 3, 1931, aged 82. And below, Charles Chaplin, died February 27, 1932. Had life turned out otherwise for the Chaplin family, both Spencer's son, Charles, and in turn his off-spring our Charlie, might have seen out their lives in Finborough and today rested in the same churchyard, two more members of a long and honourable line. As it was, I couldn't help wondering how this Charles Chaplin must have felt living in his peaceful Suffolk backwater during the early decades of the century, as the cousin who shared his name – and who he had never met, nor was ever to do so – became a world famous personality?

It was a salutory example of the vageries of fate, I thought, as I retraced my steps through the churchyard and then drove away from Great Finborough, 'seat' of the Chaplins . . .

The lack of a birth certificate for Charles Spencer Chaplin (he was given the middle name after his grandfather) has also led to confusion as to *where* precisely he was born and, indeed, on *what* day! His parents were the aforementioned Charles, who by 1889 had followed his bent to become an entertainer and was working the music halls, and his mother, Hannah Chaplin, who had been born Hannah Harriet Hill on August 6, 1865, in Walworth, and was also a singer using the name Lily Harley. By all accounts the life of the couple was unstable and often penurous, engagements frequently keeping them apart for weeks at a time, and Hannah gave birth to the young Charlie when her husband was away from home appearing at Hull.

Charlie has stated in his *Autobiogrpahy* that he was born on April 16, 1889 at East Lane, Walworth. Yet, as a glance at the map of London will show, there is *no* East Lane in Walworth. And, according to an announcement in the show business publication, The Magnet, of May 11, 1889 – and presumably inserted by his mother – the infant Chaplin was born on May 15! (Reproduced on page 12).

The precise date of his birth is, obviously, now quite impossible to establish, and the small discrepancy of twenty-four hours is only really of importance to those with an obsession about the minutiae of Chaplin's life. It is, though, possible to be much more precise about the star's *birthplace*.

The only East Lane in the vicinity of South London is to be found in Bermondsey, just off the Jamaica Road and a stone's throw from the River Thames. Today, none of the buildings that made up the mean streets of this part of dockland in 1889 still exist – in their place are several large blocks of council flats. By a curious twist of fate – considering the many comparisons drawn between Charlie's impoverished childhood and the London described by Charles Dickens who had died just 17 years earlier (to which I shall be referring later) – these flats have been named after characters from the great writer's works like Oliver House and Dorriet House. It would be somehow appropriate to declare *this* East Lane to have been Charlie's birthplace, but the facts are otherwise.

What does exist in Walworth is East *Street*, and by visiting the locality, a brisk walk down from the Elephant & Castle along the Walworth Road, it is possible to establish that this was where the star first saw the light of day. Although East Street which links the Walworth Road at one end with the Old Kent Road at the other, is clearly enough named, to the local people it has always been known as 'The Lane' because of its famous street market which has thrived for a hundred years and more and is still in existence today. It is readily understandable, therefore, why Charlie should have chosen to refer to the road as East Lane.

Although the locality is undoubtedly changed from the days when Charlie was a boy, it is still a colourful bustle of stallholders,

East Street where Charlie was born as it is today.

191, East Street – the house where Charlie was born stood on this site.

shoppers and people, much as it must have been one hundred years ago. Though now one sees people of different ethnic backgrounds and hears many different languages being spoken, the links with the past are to be found in the variety of stalls and shops (there is a winkle stall such as Charlie once frequented and a dress shop appropriately called Copperfield's), the cheerful pubs and the Robert Browning Primary School where the children play with the same kind of noisy exhuberance that youngsters have always had.

There is even a small mission hall, The Richmond Street Mission, which first opened its doors in May 1896, when Charlie was still a child, and looking over this building, I was reminded of a story the star once told about an appearance he made as a child in a mission hall. Could it have been *this* one, I wondered?

The story, which Chaplin related to journalist Victor Thompson in 1957, described how he had been moved to tears by a local missionary preaching the Gospel of salvation. 'I was about nine at the time and I have always been a bit shy about the episode because, to tell the truth, I was a flop. But I was so moved that I wanted to give Testimony in front of all the people about being saved. But when the moment came all I could stutter was, "I am so happy, so happy." The crowd burst out laughing at me and I felt so ashamed. That was really my *first* public appearance!'

Whether this event occurred at the Richmond Street Mission or not, the place stands close to the site of Chaplin's birthplace: 191, East Street. This is not only the location I had confirmed to me by local residents, but also the one accepted by Southwark Council and investigators of the British Music Hall Society.

It was in a turning off East Street, at 57, Brandon Street, that Charlie's elder brother, Sydney Chaplin, had been born four years earlier, and a number of Hannah's relatives lived in the neighbourhood. Where more natural for her to have her second child with her husband away so much, than close to her family?

There is no doubt the Chaplin's were only tenants in 191, and because of the precarious nature of their occupations (undermined by husband Charles' increasing dependence on the bottle, a dependency that was eventually to kill him), they may well have only stayed there a short time. This is also a likely explanation as to why at least three other addresses have been advanced as Charlie's birthplace. The first of these is King's Arch Place, which once ran parallel with East Street, but since demolished. Then comes Braganza Street, which runs off the Kennington Road by Kennington Underground Station, and though once full of towering old houses, has now been redeveloped with modern properties of the 'bijou' type! A third birthplace was given, by Charlie's London writer friend Thomas Burke, as Chester Street, which ran between Kennington Road and Lower Kennington Lane.

East Street, at the section where 191 stands, suffers rather from the debris of the market carried along the road and pavements, and it is not difficult to imagine that a century ago it was far less salubrious. It was the memories of this area then – as well as the other murky streets with their ramshackle houses in Walworth and Kennington which he frequented – that Chaplin drew upon

West Square, the more prosperous neighbourhood where the Chaplin family moved shortly after Charlie's birth.

for the slum street that forms the background of one of his most famous movies, *Easy Street*. Indeed, there are many others of his pictures that are coloured by his London childhood.

It was certainly not long before Hannah and her two children moved on from East Street to a rather more prosperous address at West Square, just off the Elephant & Castle. Though much of the surrounding area is run-down, West Square was then – as it is now – a pleasant oasis of terraced houses looking out over a small well maintained park.

From here, Hannah next moved to a garret at 3, Pownall Terrace, just off the Kennington Road, a place of which Charlie retained the strongest memories and which he actually returned to visit on one of his trips to London, as I have quoted later in this book. A typical memory was this one he gave to Paul Holt of the *Daily Herald* in 1952:

'I shall always remember that top room where I lived as a boy. I remember how I had to climb up and down three flights of narrow stairs to empty the buckets of troublesome slops. And nearby there was Heeley's the greengrocers where you could buy 14 llbs of coal and a penn'orth of pot herbs. You could get a pound of tuppeny pieces at Waghorn's the butcher's; and Ash's the grocer's where they sold a pennyworth of mixed stale cake, with all its pleasant and dubious surprises . . .'

A photograph taken in 1931 of 3, Pownall Terrace, Kennington, now demolished, which has frequently been cited as Charlie's birthplace.

It is perhaps not altogether surprising that because of such nostalgic quotes a considerable number of biographies have referred to Pownall Terrace as Chaplin's birthplace. I believe the real reason for him talking about it so vividly was simply because he lived there for longer than at any of the other addresses!

Sadly, apart from a few fading photographs, no trace of this property exists, because the whole terrace was bulldozed by developers in 1966 to make way for GLC houses. (Ironically, too, the owners of the property who sold it to the council were the Granada cinema group who must have screened countless films by its former tenant! Perhaps, though, the thing that would have brought a smile to Charlie's face was the fact that during the last months prior to demolition, the rooms became home for a number of tramps!)

One further London address is closely associated with Charlie's early days and has similarly been mistakenly called his birthplace: 287, Kennington Road, where actually Charlie and his brother came to live in 1898 with their father and the woman for whom he had deserted their mother. Curiously, this address, a short walk from The Oval cricket ground, is the only address to be marked with a Blue Plaque commemorating Chaplin's residency.

It is interesting to note that it was while living here that Charlie became fascinated by cricket and developed a passion for the game that remained with him all his life, despite the fact he spent much of it away from England. This little-known fact about the star was revealed by the doyen of sports writers, E. W. Swanton, while celebrating his 80th birthday in 1987.

'Most people would probably be surprised to learn Charlie Chaplin was interested in cricket,' said Swanton, 'but in fact he was potty about it. It all stemmed from his childhood growing up near The Oval. Because he had no money, he had to dodge the gatekeepers to get in to watch matches. He told me his heroes were Jack Hobbs and Bobby Abel.'

Perhaps the most easily visible tribute to Chaplin's birth in this corner of London is the public house which bears his name at the Elephant & Castle. This friendly tavern with its wooden floor and walls covered with framed stills of Charlie from his most famous pictures is a natural attraction for tourists. Appropriately, it is located next door to a cinema – and on the May day when my wife and I once again were walking the places where the young Chaplin had grown up – the choice of picture that was being shown made us both smile. The movie that was playing featured one of the new generation of comics in the Chaplin tradition, Robert Townsend. And its title was . . . *Hollywood Shuffle*!

The most puzzling mystery concerning the birth of Charlie Chaplin is undoubtedly the persistent story that he was Jewish. He himself once suggested that his origins *might* be Jewish and indeed in 1907 he actually tried to appear as a Jewish comedian at the Foresters' Music Hall, but was booed from the stage. Later, of course, he was triumphantly successful as the Jewish barber in *The Great Dictator*. There have also been a number of people close to him who were convinced he was a Jew. Again, it is an

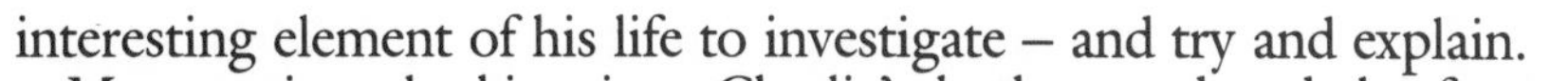

interesting element of his life to investigate – and try and explain.

Many writers looking into Charlie's background and the frustrating lack of a birth certificate must have felt like Raoul Sobel and David Francis who wrote in their *Chaplin: Genesis of a Clown* (1977): 'There is still no explanation as to why his birth is not recorded in Somerset House. It may well be that it is there under a different name.'

What a wealth of possibilities such a suggestion throws up! But, sadly, in ploughing through all the mass of material that exists about Chaplin only one alternate name comes to light: Thonstein.

There are two sources that have suggested that Charlie's real name is Thonstein. The first, and most important, of these is the authoritative German bibliographical volume, *Judisches Lexikon*, published in Berlin in 1927 and listing all the important Jews in the world. The entry for CHAPLIN, CHARLES SPENCER (reproduced here) describes him as the son of 'Charles and Hannah Thonstein, known professionally as Charles Chaplin and Lily Harley. The Thonstein family came to London in 1850 from Eastern Europe.'

The Charlie Chaplin public house at the Elephant & Castle which commemorates the area's most famous son.

The second reference appears in the 1935 edition of the *Biographical Encyclopedia of American Jews* which repeats essentially the same information as the *Judisches Lexikon*. Two further sources are cited in both entries as substantiating the claim: Jim Tully and Arnold Ulitz.

Tully was a writer who after years of poverty and survival on the road as a tramp had written a book *Beggars of Life* about his experiences which had got him an introduction to the 'little tramp' in 1920. Charlie took an immediate liking to the big, bluff American and offered him work in his studio.

During their association, the two men found much in common, especially their poverty-striken childhoods, and consequently Charlie confided many things to Tully that he told no one else. Their friendship came to an abrupt end in 1927 after Tully published a series of newspaper articles about Chaplin's life, and despite their intimacy, Charlie mentioned not one word about Jim Tully in his autobiography.

It is arguable as to just *what* it was in Tully's series that so upset Charlie – was he angry that his friend had revealed too much about his past in intimating that he has Jewish? Or did he, perhaps understandably, object to reading about himself 'husbanding his money as carefully as any Jewish moneylender'?

The German, Arnold Ulitz, was one of the first Europeans to write seriously of Charlie's talent and for this reason gained his ear in Hollywood. In 1926 he published a newspaper series 'On Chaplin' in Berlin which again highlighted Charlie's apparently Jewish origins, though not in the most favourable light. It is probably unlikely, though, that Chaplin read these reports, since they only appeared in German.

R.J. Minney, a British journalist who similarly got to know the star in Hollywood in the early years of his triumph, wrote a perceptive biography of him entitled *Chaplin: The Immortal Tramp* (1954) in which he claimed to have done considerable research into Charlie's origins and declared, 'He is partly French, partly Jewish in ancestry, with a considerable intermingling of English blood.'

Minney maintained that the ancestry came from Chaplin's mother, 'a dancer, soft-eyed, raven-haired, with all the mercurial passion of the Jewish race.'

Two other people who also knew Charlie have added further weight to this contention. The first was the boxer, Kid Lewis, who had been born in the East End of London and fought his way to the Welterweight Championship of the World by the time he was twenty. As a child he had lived in the same neighbourhood as Charlie.

In an interview in December 1930, Kid Lewis said, 'Despite my golden hair and pink skin, I'm a Jew. So is my friend Charlie Chaplin with whom I went to school. Later, when he was working for Fred Karno he got me a job as a scene shifter. Sometimes we used to go out at night together and fool around and always end up at a coffee stall. Oh, those were great days. We neither of us thought we'd be famous.'

One of Charlie's fellow actors with Fred Karno was Chester

JÜDISCHES LEXIKON

Ein enzyklopädisches Handbuch des jüdischen Wissens in vier Bänden

Begründet von

Dr. Georg HERLITZ und Dr. Bruno KIRSCHNER

Mit über 2000 Illustrationen, Beilagen, Karten und Tabellen

*

Unter Mitarbeit von über 250 jüdischen Gelehrten und Schriftstellern

und unter redaktioneller Mithilfe von

Prof. Dr. Ismar ELBOGEN / Dr. Georg HERLITZ / Dr. Josef MEISL
Dr. Aron SANDLER / Dr. Max SOLOWEITSCHIK / Dr. Felix A. THEILHABER / Dr. Robert WELTSCH / Rabb. Dr. Max WIENER

BAND I

A—C

JVB

JÜDISCHER VERLAG / BERLIN

1329 Chaplin, Charles Spencer — Charter 1330

CHAPLIN, CHARLES SPENCER, einer der berühmtesten Filmschauspieler der Gegenwart, geb. 1889 in London als Sohn einer Mitte des 19. Jhdts. in England eingewanderten Ostjudenfamilie, die urspr. den Namen Thonstein führte, wanderte neunzehnjährig nach Amerika aus und wurde Mitglied einer zweitrangigen Varieté-Truppe. Durch den Filmunternehmer Mac Sennet in Los-Angeles kam er zum Film und wurde bald der Liebling des amerikanischen Publikums und in der Folge weltbekannt. Ch. ist Verfasser, Regisseur und Hauptdarsteller der meisten seiner Filme („Goldrausch", „Hundeleben", „Pariser Frauen"). Seine Stärke liegt — von seiner hervorragenden Mimik und geschickten Spiegelung der spezifisch amerikanischen Komik, die aus dem ständigen Kampfe mit der Tücke des Objekts fließt, abgesehen — in der Fähigkeit, plötzlich mitten im vermeintlichen Scherz durch Darstellung hoffnungsloser Schwermut, zeitloser, jüdisch anmutender Tragik und stummer Verzweiflung bis ins Innerste zu erschüttern. Ch. zeichnet sich durch große Wohltätigkeit und Förderung anderer Talente aus; so entdeckte er u. a. die Filmtalente Jackie Coogan und Adolphe Menjou.

Lit.: Jim Tully, „Charlie Chaplin" (Prager Tagblatt 24., 28. IV., 6., 11. V. 1927); Arnold Ulitz' Gedicht „An Chaplin" (Berl. Tageblatt im Nov. 1926).

L. D.

Charausses s. Seder.

CHARIF (aram. חָרִיף) = „scharfsinnig", „geistreich". Davon *Charifut* oder *Charifuss* (חֲרִיפוּת): 1. Scharfsinn; 2. geistvolle Bemerkung (s. auch Baki). Ch. wurde *Ehrentitel zahlreicher rabbinischer Gelehrten.

E. E. B.

Charifuss, Charifut s. Charif.

CHARIMSEL, vulg. auch Chrimsel (Krimsel), eine besonders zu *Pessach bei Juden beliebte Mehlspeise aus *Mazza-Mehl, Eiern, Rosinen, Zucker und einem Zusatz von Fett hergestellt. Der Name stammt wohl aus dem Slawischen.

E. W. L.

Charisi s. Juda alcharisi.

CHARKOWER KONFERENZ. Im Okt. 1903 fand in Charkow eine von M. *Ussischkin veranlaßte Konferenz führender russischer Zionisten, insb. von Mitgliedern des Großen Aktions-Komitees der *Zionistischen Organisation, statt, die den Beschluß faßte, von *Herzl, dem Präsidenten der Organisation, die schriftliche Erklärung zu fordern, daß er das Ostafrika-Projekt (s. Uganda) definitiv aufgeben, den späteren *Zionistenkongressen keine weiteren, nicht Palästina betreffenden Projekte vorlegen und in eine praktische Palästina-Arbeit einwilligen werde. Sollte der Führer diese Forderungen ablehnen, so wollten die Konferenz-Teilnehmer eine zionistische Sonderorganisation in Rußland begründen. Eine nach Wien entsandte Deputation sollte Herzl dieses Ultimatum vorlegen. Dieser, damals schon schwer leidend, war aufs tiefste über dieses Vorgehen verletzt und weigerte sich, die Deputation zu empfangen. Er ließ sie nur als Gäste an einer Sitzung des „Engeren Aktions-Komitees" (s. Zionismus, Organisation) teilnehmen. Zu einer eingehenden Aussprache über die von den „Charkowern" angeschnittenen Fragen kam es erst bei der Sitzung des Grossen Aktions-Komitees im Apr. 1904, deren Ergebnis die Wiederherstellung des Friedens und der Einheit der Organisation war. Die Gemüter beruhigten sich, nachdem man erkannt hatte, daß es eine politische Ehrenpflicht der Organisation sei, die vom Kongreß beschlossene Expedition nach Ostafrika zu entsenden, daß aber niemand an ein Aufgeben Palästinas denke. Die Entscheidung über die Frage der praktischen Palästina-Arbeit wurde bis zur nächsten Sitzung des Großen Aktions-Komitees verschoben, die dann aber nicht mehr zu Lebzeiten Herzls stattfand. S. im übr. Zionismus, Neuere Zeit.

Lit.: A. Böhm, Die zionistische Bewegung; M. Ussischkin, Unser Programm; Die Wahrheit über Ch., 1904.

W. H. Sch.

Charoschet-Hagojim s. Kolonien, landwirtschaftliche, in Palästina.

Charosset s. Seder.

Charot(d)e s. Vulgärausdrücke.

CHARTER (vom lat. charta, Freibrief). Im modernen englischen Staatsrecht wird unter Chartered Company eine mit einem Schutzbrief ausgestattete Landgesellschaft verstanden, insb. die Britisch-Südafrikanische Gesellschaft. Der Charter wird erteilt zum Zweck der Erwerbung und Verwaltung von Land, das noch nicht dem Reich gehört. *Herzl gebraucht seit dem 3. *Zionistenkongreß das Wort für die vom Sultan zu erteilende und von den Großmächten zu garantierende Urkunde, wonach den *Zionisten unter türkischer Souveränität die Selbstverwaltung Palästinas übertragen werden sollte. Analog wird „Charter" später für die erhoffte Vertragsurkunde bezüglich der Gebiete von *El-Arisch und Nairobi (Brit. Ost-Afrika) verwendet. Mehrere Charterentwürfe sind von Herzl selbst angefertigt worden. Die Frage des Ch. führte zu leidenschaftlichen Meinungskämpfen, da auch nach Herzls Tode die „Charteristen" jede größere Kolonisations-Arbeit in Palästina vor Erlangung des Ch. als wertlos verwarfen. Sie sind schließlich unterlegen (1907 auf d. 8. *Zionistenkongreß), aber auch später, nachdem selbst *Nordau nach der türki-

The entry in the *Judisches Lexikon* of 1927 which started the mystery about Charlie's allegedly Jewish origins.

Courtney, who strongly suspected Charlie had Jewish origins. Being interviewed in March 1931, Courtney said: 'The only invitation I ever knew him to accept once he had become famous in Hollywood was that of an old Jewish lady who asked him to attend a baby show at the Boston Stores in Los Angeles. He spent the day in the store, carried Hebrew babies in his arms, and wound up by collecting a thousand dollars for the foundling home.'

There are other examples of what have been advanced as further proof of Chaplin's Jewish ancestry (Gabriel Blanco's article 'Charlot Juif' in the French magazine *Ecran*, June 1977 makes interesting reading) but I am convinced the truth of the matter lies in a simple case of misunderstanding – and brings this piece of research back full circle to Great Finborough in Suffolk.

Before offering my conclusion, I should just mention that the resourceful W.O.G. Lofts has scoured all the appropriate registers in London in the hope of finding some trace of the elusive Thonsteins, but no such name is on record at any period even remotely near that of Charles Chaplin or his ancestors. As he reported to me, 'Certainly as far as the official records go there is no evidence of a Jewish connection or the name Thonstein. It is possible that going back some generations a family of that name could have come from Europe and changed their name to Chaplin. But Chaplin is a very old English name, sometimes spelt Chaplain, when it has been found recorded in Devon as early as the 12th century. There is absolutely no concrete evidence I have been

able to locate that our Charles Chaplin was directly descended from anything other than pure English stock.'

What I believe to be the vital clue to the mystery lies in the Chaplin family's use of Old Testament names such as Shadrach, Meshach and Abednego. It seems quite feasible to me that Charlie heard mention of these names – in particular that of his great-great-grandfather Meshach – and wondered if his forebears had been Jews. As someone who made the most of all the colourful facts he could find relating to himself in the creation of his legend, such names were surely just too good to be overlooked?

I suspect, though, that the debate will go on. Even as recently as 1978, following the terrible events in Switzerland when Charlie's body was stolen from his tomb in an attempt to demand a ransom, the Jewish connection was raised once more. For just prior to the recovery of the body, one of the more sensational Hollywood tabloids reported that the coffin had been removed from the tomb 'because Chaplin was a Jew buried in a non-Jewish cemetary'!

In all the welter of debate that has taken place on this topic, there is, however, one statement that is difficult to dispute and which somehow encapsulates both Charlie's life and the nature of his great film characterisation which won the love and admiration of the whole world. The statement was made by Robert Leslie Liebman in a thought-provoking article entitled, 'Rabbis or Rakes, Schlemiels or Superman? Jewish Identity in Charles Chaplin, Jerry Lewis and Woody Allen' which appeared in *The Literature and Film Quarterly* (No 3, 1984). Liebman wrote:

'Although he was probably not Jewish (Chaplin's obscure genealogy points in non-Jewish directions), his immortal silent Tramp was. To Hannah Arendt, the Tramp is a "schlemihl" and a "little Yid". The comedian, Arendt continues, "has epitomised in an artistic form a character born of the Jewish pariah mentality." As a child, Chaplin learned the time-honoured Jewish truth that, other things being equal, the human ingenuity of a David can sometimes outmatch the animal strength of a Goliath.'

A CHILD FULL OF MONKEY BUSINESS

The earliest memories of Charlie Chaplin that I have been able to trace are those of a part-time nurse, Mrs Harriet Tricks, who was actually present at his birth in East Lane. In 1921, and then 70 years old and living in one room at 141, Ethelred Street, Kennington, the widowed lady had these comments to make:

'I was the nurse who assisted at Charlie's birth and I saw him grow up. He had a very hard life as a child.

'Many a slice of bread and butter and cup of tea I have taken out to him when I was charring at the home of Mr Wentworth, the lamp manufacturer, in Kennington Road. Mr Wentworth was then an elderly man, and is now dead, but he often found Charlie curled up asleep in his doorway.

'He was just a mischievous boy, but very funny, always up to monkey tricks, tripping himself up, climbing up fences and falling down. I remember he used to climb the fences and steal apples from the orchard of a house in Kennington Lane, in which lived an old lady who was known as "The Old Miser" because of her meanness. The house is now pulled down, but there was no doubt he could nip up her fence all right!

'He was always wonderfully fond of animals, and was a good pal to a dog.

'From what I have seen of Charlie's film, *The Kid*, there is no doubt he's playing his own life as a boy as near as possible. I can't read, but I have to form my own impressions from the pictures I see, and I have often thought to myself, "It's what he used to do and went through as a boy."

Chaplin in a scene from *The Kid*, his famous movie based on his London childhood. The child is Jackie Coogan and the Doctor, Jules Hanft.

A FAMILY ON THE MOVE

Charlie Chaplin's early days in London were unsettled and often unhappy as his mother, Hannah, having been deserted by his father, was forced to move him and his older brother, Sydney, from one cheap lodging to the next. In 1952, Mrs J. Crane, who had briefly been the family's landlady in 1898 at 39, Methley Street, Kennington, recalled their plight and how they had attempted to cope:

'Mrs Chaplin and her boys stayed at numerous addresses round and about the Horns Hotel, Kennington. Chester Street, Oakden Street, Pownall Terrace and Methley Street, many of them now gone in the blitz, were the kind of places they lived in for a few weeks when they had some money.

'The family had one attic room with me. When she couldn't get singing engagements, poor Mrs Chaplin worked all day at needlework, making blouses for a few pennies each. She had a hard job making ends meet.

'The older boy, Sydney, worked for the Post Office, I think. Charles was a rather frail child with his mop of dark hair, his pale face and bright blue eyes. He was what I call a little limb – out in the streets from morning to night.

'I remember he was a regular one for finding a man with a barrel organ and dancing to the music. He got a lot of extra money for the organ grinder and a few coppers for himself. I suppose that's how he started becoming an entertainer.

'Charlie was supposed to go to school in Kennington, but he was an awful truant.'

CHARLIE'S SCHOOLDAYS

Charlie had a very chequered education because of his unsettled home life, being moved from one South London school to another from the age of four until he was almost ten and entered the theatrical world. His very first teacher was Mrs E.E. Turner-Dauncey, who, from her retirement home in Westcliffe-on-Sea, recalled in January 1957:

'I taught Charlie Chaplin at Victory Place Board School, Walworth, when he was between four and five.

'I remember his large eyes – his mass of dark curly hair, and his beautiful small hands. He was very sweet and so shy.

'He copied his famous walk from an old man who gave oatmeal and water to the horses with cabs and carts outside the Elephant & Castle.'

That same year of 1957, Charlie himself recalled one of his teachers at the second primary school he attended, the Addington Street School in Lambeth, where he was enrolled in October 1895:

'I remember the master there, a man named Reed, and a good teacher he was, as far as anybody could be with 50 Cockney urchins in a class.

'He had a good way of keeping us in order. When our noise became impossible, he would pick up a T-square and thwack it thunderously on his desk, making a worse din than ours.

'Once he put his head back and howled like a dog. We were startled into silence!'

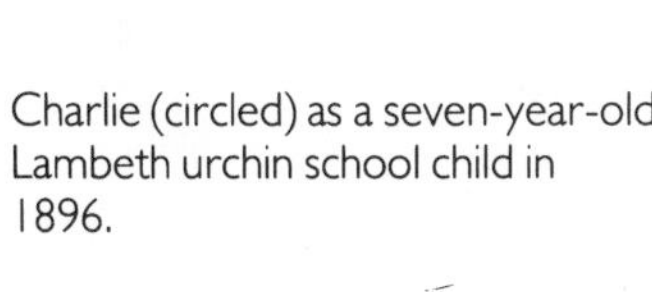

Charlie (circled) as a seven-year-old Lambeth urchin school child in 1896.

COCKNEY PALS

Among young Charlie's friends in the Walworth area was Mr W.C. Sherrington, still living near the Elephant & Castle at Paster Street when he reminisced in 1952 about the star's early days:

'Some of the lads Charlie used to get about with were Fred Ernest, Gus Elton, Fred Leslie, Harry Wharton and Nigger Heaton. They had a bit of roller shutter and practised tap-dancing on it by the Old King's Hall and at the back of the South London Palace.

'I am sure Charlie got his funny walk from the old boy who had a stall outside Crosse's, the ironmongers next door to the South London Palace. The old boy suffered from gout and had outsize boots.

'We would upset his tins and then he would come after us saying, "Pork and rabbit, you can have it," and up would come his foot, just like Charlie's does!

'I remember once when Charlie was in the Bakerloo Cafe in London Road. He was called outside by a gentleman. The lady of the cafe called to him, "Charlie, your two fried eggs and chips are ready."

'How Charlie raved at her! He said, "I may have been telling that gentleman that I was having a lunch of champagne and chicken!"

'That was Charlie every time, very quick on the uptake. Every Cockney should be proud of Charlie – he never forgot the hard times and was always ready to help the under dog.'

A fascinating comparison: an old London match seller pictured in 1905 and Charlie in his tramp costume.

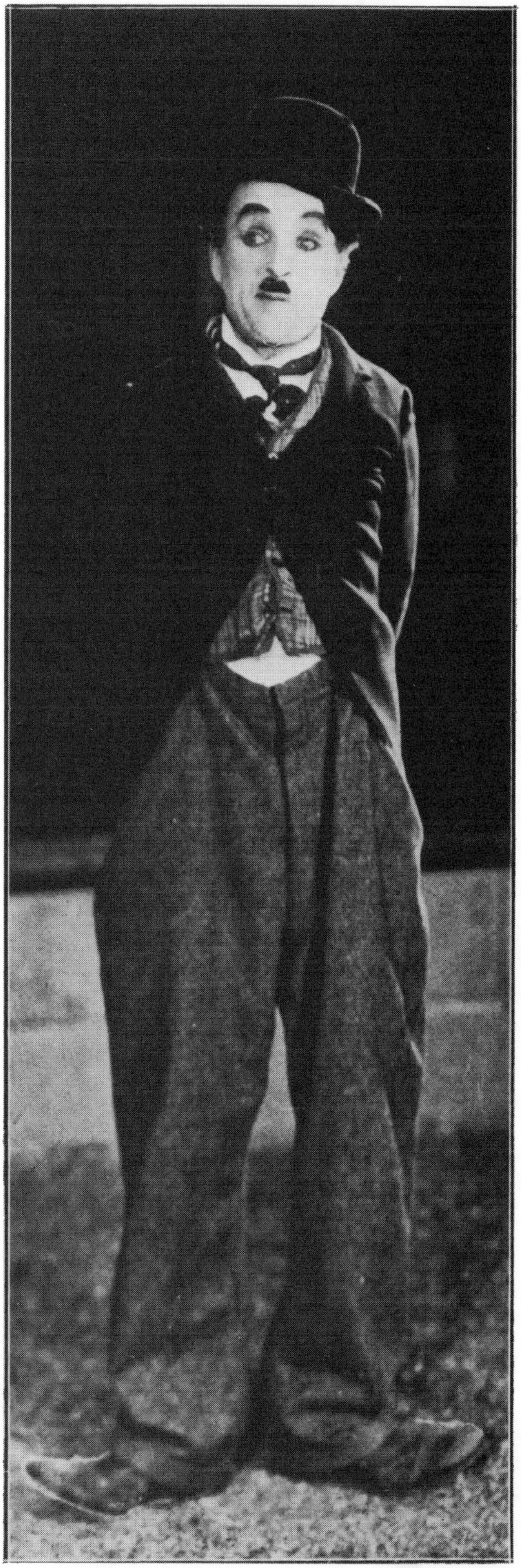

THE COMICAL INFLUENCES ON CHAPLIN

Ally Sloper, the first Victorian comic strip hero.

Charlie Chaplin was no different from any other London youngster of the turn of the nineteenth century – or today, for that matter! – in that he loved reading comics. The introduction of education for everyone coupled with the development of machinery that made inexpensive printing at last possible had lead to the appearance of the first comic paper, *Funny Folks*, in December 1874, priced at one penny. This mixture of funny stories and cartoons proved such a success that by the time young Charlie was born, there had been a veritable boom in comics, and there were several other popular titles available such as *Comic Cuts*, *The Wonder* and *Illustrated Chips*, the last-named being distinctively printed on pink paper! Their success was also due in no small measure to the fact they were a whole half penny cheaper than *Funny Folks*.

In all of these eight-page tabloid-size publications, readers discovered various strip cartoons in which stories were told either by captions underneath the line drawings or else in balloons issuing from the characters' mouths (sometimes, a combination of both). The action and text in these strips was deliberately kept simple so that even the most backward readers – as well as those who were illiterate – could understand what was going on. Small wonder that Charlie, who loved anything that was visual but had struggled to learn to read, found a wealth of pleasure and fun in such publications.

Charlie was almost certainly aware of the first comic strip hero, the extraordinary Ally Sloper, who looked like a thin version of the film star W.C. Fields, and was always just a slip away from disaster. He had been appearing in a weekly magazine called *Judy* (an unashamed rival to *Punch*) since 1867 and was something of a national institution. Ally Sloper's name was actually a pun on the Victorian expression for dodging away down an alley when the rent collector appeared, and as a small-time con-man he was forever dreaming up get-rich-quick schemes which never quite worked. For someone from young Chaplin's background, Ally Sloper would have had a strong appeal, though how often he would have had access to *Judy* at twopence per copy is debatable.

There is no doubt, however, that he was a regular reader of *Illustrated Chips*, on whose pink front page appeared the most famous of all the early comic strip heroes, Weary Willie and Tired

Tim. Just how influential these two tramps, one tall and thin and the other short and fat, and both ragged, though eternally resolute in the face of all adversity, were in Chaplin's own career is a not widely known element in the story of his life.

The tramps were created by Tom Browne, a brilliantly original cartoonist and illustrator who was born in humble circumstances in Nottingham in 1870 and evolved a style of drawing which was ideal for the new comics and in time made him one of the most 'in-demand' artists in the field. Weary Willy and Tired Tim first appeared as 'Weary Waddles and Tired Timmy' in May 1896, but so impressed the Editor of *Illustrated Chips* that he asked Browne for more adventures. Readers also shared this enthusiasm, too, and the pair of tramps went on to become the longest-lived of all British comic strip heroes, their exploits being continued by another artist, Percy Cocking, following Browne's premature death in 1910, aged just 39. Like Chaplin, Browne's work had a profound influence on the medium in which he chose to work, and his influence can still be seen today. This fact makes their association all the more fascinating, as the reader will see . . .

Weary Willie and Tired Tim – who Browne once said were based on a couple of tramps he actually saw near his London home at Blackheath – made their debut on the front of *Illustrated Chips*

Weary Willie and Tired Tim, the two tramp heroes who inspired Chaplin.

Casey's Court, the comic strip series, in which Charlie was later to appear when it was adapted for the stage.

in May 1896 when Charlie Chaplin was an energetic eight-year-old. In his book, *My Autobiography*, Charlie only mentions his love of comics in passing, commenting that one of his rare pleasures was reading 'my weekly comic on a serene Sunday morning.'

He was much more forthcoming – and revealing – in September 1957 while talking to Victor Thompson, a journalist on the *The Daily Herald*, who shared Charlie's Socialist views and wrote a number of highly sympathetic articles about him. The two men met several times in both America and Europe. One day, while they were dining together at a Riviera restaurant in the South of France, Charlie began reminiscing about his younger days – and one particular occasion when he had a short-lived job at a glass-blowing establishment in London.

'In the lunch-breaks I used to entertain the men with sand dances,' he told Thompson. 'On one occasion I danced so furiously that I got sick and had to be sent home. I sat on the kerb feeling I was dying. A woman gave me a penny to go home by horse-bus, but I walked and bought a comic with the windfall.

'Ah, those comics,' Charlie went on, 'the wonderfully vulgar papers for boys with "Casey Court" pictures in them, and the Adventures of Weary Willie and Tired Tim, two famous tramps with the world against them. There's been a lot said about how I evolved the little tramp character who made my name. Deep, psychological stuff has been written about how I meant him to be a symbol of the class war, of the love-hate concept, the death wish and what-all.

'But if you want the simple Chaplin truth behind the Chaplin legend, I started the little tramp simply to make people laugh and because those other old tramps, Weary Willie and Tired Tim, had always made me laugh.'

Victor Thompson was clearly moved by Charlie's revelation that the inspiration for his immortal creation had come from the pages of a children's comic, and closed his article: 'We went back

in Charles' Bentley to the villa where he was staying. We should have had two cigars each – as Weary Willie and Tired Tim did in the last picture of their weekly adventures!'

Glancing through old copies of *Illustrated Chips* from the 1890s it is possible to find similarities between the scrapes that Weary Willie and Tired Tim got into and some of Charlie's later films: even the titles of some of the early movies seem derived from the adventures of the comic strip heroes. And if further proof of the influence is needed, the very appearance of the gaunt Weary Willie is surely strikingly similar to that of Chaplin's Little Tramp?

Also to be found in the pages of *Illustrated Chips* is the other series to which Charlie refered in his chat with Victor Thompson: "Casey Court". This took the form of a single giant panel in which a gang of back street London urchins were depicted in chaotic action. Foremost among these was Billy Baggs, the leader of the boys who existed in a kind of uneasy alliance with the leader of the girls, Sally Trotters. Billy Baggs was undoubtedly Charlie's hero.

The youngsters were the creation of Julius Stafford Baker, himself a former London slum child, and made the first of what were to be over 2,300 appearances in May 1902. As in the case of Tom Browne's two tramps, once Baker gave up drawing the urchins, others took over their adventures, including Louis Briault and Charlie Pease.

What made the series such a success with readers was its topicality – the Casey Court gang mimicking new inventions, leading social gatherings, even – in 1913 – the threat of invasion, all done in their own inimitable way. Charlie undoubtedly saw much in these panels that mirrored his own childhood in the means streets of South London.

In fact, so popular did 'Casey Court' become that in 1905 the pantomime comedian, Will Murray, transferred the idea to the stage playing himself 'Mrs Casey'. It was described as 'a street urchin's idea of life' and was set in the requisite alley where Murray was joined in high spirited action by a dozen juvenile comedians. Following a successful run, Murray produced a sequel, 'Casey's Court Circus' which opened in Liverpool in May 1906.

Just prior to this, the production was advertised in *The Era* with the information that boy comedians were required. Not surprisingly, Charlie, the young actor who had been reared on the comic strip, was quick to apply, having been out of work since the end of a 'Sherlock Holmes' tour in March. To his delight, he so impressed Will Murray that the comedian handed him the coveted role of none other than his hero, Billy Baggs! He remained with 'Casey's Court Circus' for a year until it closed in July 1907.

The comedian, Will Murray, later recalled that Chaplin was a keen comic reader and was clearly familiar with the 'Casey Court' strip in *Illustrated Chips*. Explaining how the boy came into his production, he said:

'To carry out a second edition of the sketch, I found it necessary to advertise for a number of boys between 14 and 19 years of age. Amongst the applicants was one little lad who took my fancy at once. I asked him his name and what theatrical experience he had.

An article by the founder of Casey's Court, Will Murray, from the *Weekly Record* of September 10, 1921.

HOW I DISCOVERED CHAPLIN

Amusing Incidents in the Early Career of the Great Little Comedian.

CHARLIE AT WORK AND AT PLAY.

By Will Murray of "Casey's Court" Fame.

FORTUNE delights in playing strange pranks with we poor human creatures.

One of her favourites—and the world's favourite, too—is Charlie Chaplin, whose title to fame it would be ridiculous to specify.

When Charlie again lands on his native shores, the monarch's welcome that he certainly will receive will contrast strangely with his quiet, unnoticed departure for the Eldorado of the West not so many years ago.

I first met Charlie when I was running the sketch "Casey's Court (Circus)." These sketches, which were pure burlesque, met with a great measure of success throughout the country.

To carry out a second edition of the sketch, I found it necessary to advertise for a number of boys between fourteen and nineteen years of age.

Amongst the applicants was one little lad who took my fancy at once. I asked him his name and what theatrical experience he had had.

"Charlie Chaplin, sir," was the reply. "I've been one of the Eight Lancashire Lads, and just now I've got a part in the sketch 'Sherlock Holmes.'"

I put him through his paces. He sang, danced, and did a little of practically everything in the entertaining line. He had the makings of a "star" in him, and I promptly took him on—salary, 30s per week.

Included amongst the subjects we burlesqued were several famous music-hall stars. I particularly wanted a good thing made of Dr. Bodie. Chaplin seemed the likeliest of the lot for the part, and he got it.

Rehearsals were numerous, and Charlie always showed a keen desire to learn. He had never seen Bodie's turn, but I endeavoured to give him an idea of the Doctor's little mannerisms.

For hours he would practise these in front of a mirror. He would walk for long spells backwards and forwards cultivating the Bodie manner.

Then he would ring the changes with a characteristic twist to the Bodie moustache, the long, flowing adornment which the "Electric Spark" affected, not the now world-famous tooth-brush variety.

In addition, Charlie was the principal in another burlesque, "Dick Turpin."

His first appearance with "Casey's Court" was at the Olympia, Liverpool, and he "got" the audience right away with "Dr. Bodie."

Then came "Dick Turpin," that old invincible ever-green standby of the circus. It all went well, but the climax was the fight after the death of "Bonnie Black Bess."

You can imagine the position of poor Mr. Turpin. He had to run, hide, do anything to get out of the way of the runners, and yet he had nowhere to go except round the circus track.

Nevertheless, Charlie started to run—and run—and run. He had to turn innumerable corners, and as he raised one foot and hopped along a little way on the other in getting round a nasty "bend" the audience simply howled.

I think it can justly be said that I am the man who taught Charlie to turn corners. Yes, that peculiar run, and still more weird one-leg turning of corners, which seems so simple when you see it carried out in the pictures, is the very same manœuvre that I taught Chaplin to go through in the burlesque of Dick Turpin.

It took many, many weary hours of monotonous rehearsals, but I am sure Charlie Chaplin, in looking back over those hours of rehearsals, will thank me for being so persistent in my instructions as to how I wanted the thing done.

I remember one evening the front row of the stalls was occupied by a party of ladies and gentlemen. I noticed that they were deeply interested in the doings of the young actors, and that when Charlie came on they paid special attention to him.

They encored him again and again, and after the show sent round a message, and he was utterly taken aback. In those days callers at the theatre were few and far between, and it was a tremendous honour for anyone—especially among the would-be stars—to have a card sent round. Charlie recounted the conversation he had there to me afterwards.

"You're very young," the lady said to him. "Yes," replied Charlie, giving her his correct age. "Dear me," she went on, "I have never seen anything like your impersonation of Dr Bodie in all my life. I ought to know, for I have known him all my life."

But others in the profession weren't long in seeing that there was a great future before the lad. Fred Karno was one of them, and he offered Charlie an engagement at £2 a week.

Charlie came and told me; so, desirous of keeping him with me, I said I would give him £3.

But Karno was keen on the boy, so the game of increasing the offers went on.

One day Charlie told me that Karno had offered him £6.

"Well, Chaplin," I said. "I'm afraid I can't afford to pay you that, so you'll better take the chance you're being offered."

He started as a "super" in the sketch "Stiffy the Goalkeeper," the leading role of which was being filled by Harry Weldon.

During the run at the Liverpool Olympia, Harry became indisposed, and Karno told Charlie that he was to understudy for "Stiffy," and so well did he fill the role that at the end of the run he was given a part in "The Mumming Birds" when he caught the eye of most of the discriminating comedy "fans."

One little incident during Chaplin's stay with me always comes back. It happened when we were appearing at the Empire Theatre, Nottingham, in 1907.

The races were on, and poor old 'Gene Stratton, the greatest coon comedian that ever faced the footlights, gave me a sure tip.

It was Renzo, Danny Maher's first mount after his motor accident. I decided to go to the meeting, and Charlie asked if he could come with me.

Just before the start of the second, he came up to me and asked if I could loan him 6d.

"What for?" I asked. "Well, I've got a sure thing for the race, and I've only got a 'tanner.'"

"I'll go down, too," I said.

"Not at all," he replied. "This is bound to win."

"Oh, I queried, "what's its name?"

He said it was Bobarinsky. (I don't know if that is how it's spelt, but that's what it sounded like.) In the end he put the bob on.

When the horses came into the straight, Bobarinsky was leading by a couple of lengths.

Charlie became so excited that he scrambled up the rails, shouting "Bobarinsky! Bobarinsky!" at the pitch of his voice.

A lady standing near said to me, "How excited the young man is. He must have a lot of money on the horse."

"He has," I replied, "Sixpence of mine and sixpence of his own." And Bobarinsky didn't win after all.

Well, we're all scattered now, and I myself am appearing in Henry Lee's revue, "Froth," which comes to the Glasgow Coliseum in a fortnight's time.

(1) Charlie Chaplin at the age of sixteen; and (2) Mr. Will Murray, of "Casey's Court" fame, who discovered the great little comedian.

A special illustrated article on why Charlie Chaplin came home appears on page 18 of this issue.

'Charlie Chaplin, sir' was the reply. 'I've been one of the Eight Lancashire Lads of clog dancers, and just now I had a part in Sherlock Holmes.' I put him through his paces. He sang, danced and did a little of practically everything in the entertaining line. He had the makings of a star in him, and I promptly took him on.' (Interestingly, another young comic who was to become a famous film star was employed for in time in the 'Casey Court' series – Stan Laurel.)

In his autobiography, Charlie refers only briefly to 'Casey's Court Circus' – and not very flatteringly. 'I was the star of the company, and earned three pounds a week. It included a troupe of kids playing at grown-ups in an alley scene; it was an awful show, I thought, but it gave me a chance to develop as a comedian.'

Charlie's love of comics has been recalled by others who knew him, too. Alfred Reeves, who became Chaplin's manager in 1910, described the first performance in which he saw him with the Fred Karno troupe as that of 'a dime-novel struck errand boy forever reading Wild West blood-and-thunder thrillers.'

The star's eldest son, Charles Chaplin jnr has likewise recalled that, apart from comics, his father also liked pulp magazines. Writing in *My Father, Charlie Chaplin* (1960), the son says: 'I recall the pulp detective magazines that were always stacked by his bed. My father might read Spengler and Schopenhauer and Kant for edification, but for sheer relaxation he chose murder mysteries. Tired from a hard day's work, he liked to read them in bed for they put him to sleep.'

Although the younger Chaplin does not name these magazines, it seems a fair bet that the long-running adventures of the rugged crime-buster Nick Carter were among these, as Charlie specifically refers in his autobiography to the town of Butte, Montana in 1910 as being 'still a Nick Carter town, with miners wearing top-boots and two gallon hats and red neckerchiefs.' It was there that Chaplin actually watched a gun battle between a sheriff and an escaped prisoner which could have come straight from the pages of one of the blood-and-thunder magazines he read!

It seems not only appropriate, but also rather predictable, that as Charlie Chaplin had found inspiration from the comics, when fame came his way, he in turn was featured as a cartoon character in those self-same publications. As early as 1915 the Little Tramp made his debut in strip cartoon form, and he has been featured in this manner ever since: most recently as the star of an animated TV cartoon series.

The comic which first brought Charlie to young readers was the successor to one of the publications that he himself had read, *The Wonder*. This paper, *The Funny Wonder* was launched in February 1893, and, taking a leaf from *Illustrated Chips*, was printed on green paper. It ran to eight pages and sold for one halfpenny.

'Charlie Chaplin – The Scream of the Earth' the strip was headlined on the front page of the green paper in August 1915, with a message from the Editor which declared, 'Here he is, folks!

1

2

3

The French adventures of Charlot drawn by Jean Thomen from 1918.

Charlie becomes a cartoon strip hero himself – an illustration by Albert Brown from the first appearance of 'The Scream of the Earth' in *The Funny Wonder*, August 7, 1915.

Jackie Coogan co-starring with Charlie in *The Funny Wonder* of July 5, 1924.

An oddly-dressed Charlie with Luke the Gook in the American cartoon strip drawn by E.C. Segar which started in 1915.

Good old Charlie! Absolutely IT! A scream from start to finish!' The strip was drawn by the versatile Albert 'Bertie' Brown who was given free range to invent all sorts of escapades for Charlie, many of which consisted of him outwitting some villain or unscrupulous snob and getting the girl.

Following the success of *The Kid* in 1921, Charlie gained a partner in his adventures in the shape of the young Jackie Coogan – an obvious ploy to provide young readers with a point of identification. The series in *Funny Wonder* lasted until May 1944, when Charlie took his leave under a billing which described him topically as 'The Great Dictator of Laughter.'

America was only slightly behind Britain in featuring Charlie Chaplin in cartoon form. 'Charlie Chaplin's Comic Capers' first appeared in late 1915 in the *Chicago Record-Herald* (later *The Chicago Herald*), drawn by a young man named E.C. Segar, who was later to become famous as the creator of Popeye. The five-panel adventures of Charlie appeared daily in the newspaper and mostly consisted of verbal exchanges between the comedian and a diminutive companion named Luke the Gook. Curiously, Charlie appeared in many of these strips wearing only a waistcoat and no jacket, shirt or tie!

In Europe, the French were the first to capitalise on the popularity of Chaplin in comic strip form when Jean Thomen, an imaginative newspaper illustrator, began *Les Aventures Acrobatiques de Charlot* in 1918. First syndicated to several regional newspapers, the strips later appeared in booklet format and are now much sought-after collectors' items.

An interesting off-shoot of the success of these comic strips occurred in Britain when a series of fictionalisations of the Chaplin films, complete with cartoon illustrations, began to appear in the top-selling weekly magazine, *The Family Journal*, in September 1915. These were written by Langford Reed, a former scriptwriter, who had become Chaplin's publicist in Britain. Later, Reed was to write and direct a compilation film of extracts from his boss's movies called *Chase Me Charlie* (1917), in which linking scenes were filmed with an actor called Graham Douglas impersonating the Little Tramp. The fictionalisations by Langford Reed gave the outline of the film's story, but in such an abbreviated form as not to spoil the pleasure of any prospective cinema-goer.

It has to be said in hindsight that is doubtful whether Chaplin saw much of this 'cartooning' of his life: for the strips in *Funny Wonder*, for example, were unauthorised, as were many of the others which appeared in places as far apart as Germany and Japan in the immediate aftermath of his meteoric rise to frame. But those examples which later found their way into his archives must have afforded him at least a smile of pleasure if no extra cash. For if nothing else, they were surely a reminder of the debt he himself owed to the comic strip for inspiring his rise to fame.

A NIPPER ON THE STAGE

Charlie was nine years old when he got his first theatrical job with the clog dancing troupe, 'The Eight Lancashire Lads', and he toured with them on and off for a couple of years from Christmas 1898. A friend from this period of his life was Bert Herbert, who later became a professional comedian himself, and in 1921 while living at Wolsey Road, Leyton, reminisced about his pal:

A dapper looking Charlie (centre) with other members of the cast of Casey's Court in 1906.

'My introduction to Charlie Chaplin was through my uncle. After Charlie had left 'The Eight Lancashire Lads', my uncle brought him to our house in Thrush Street, Walworth, and asked my parents if they would agree to my brother and I joining this boy to tour as a dancing trio.

'My people agreed, and Charlie took over his duties straight away. He was an excellent dancer and teacher, but I am afraid we did more larking about than dancing – we were all between 10- and 14-years-old. Eventually we mastered six steps (the old six Lancashire steps) and got a trial show at the Montpelier in Walworth, of which at that time I believe a Mr Ben Weston was the proprietor.

'I remember that we had no stage dresses, and went on in our street clothes. Charlie and my brother wore knickerbockers, and as I had long trousers I had to tie them up underneath at the knee to make them look like knickers. How Charlie laughed when I went wrong, because one leg of my trousers started to come down as soon as I commenced to dance!

'My uncle then went to America, and as we had no money to carry on, we had to let the trio fall through. It was to have been called "Ted Prince's Nippers".

'I lost sight of Charlie for some time then, but I met him again when he was with Mr Murray in 'Casey's Court'. At the time I am speaking of, Charlie lived in the buildings in Munton Road, off the New Kent Road. He certainly was not a 'gutter snipe' as some people have said. In fact, my mother used to admonish my brother and I with the remark, "Why aren't you good like little Charlie? See how clean he keeps himself and how well behaved he is!"

'Of course, I could have told her that he was as bad as us when she was out of the way, but then, as now, he could pull the innocent face at a second's notice.

'I have heard it said that Charlie was always funny as a boy, but, on the contrary, I found him just the reverse. I think he himself would bear out my statement. His one ambition was to be a villain in drama. We often used to act a drama in the kitchen, and Charlie always wanted to be the villain. He certainly did not have awkward feet, as some people have suggested.

'He was an ingenious kid. I remember often going to his house in Munton Road and playing with a farthing in the slot machine which he had made. It was an exact miniature model of the penny in the slot machines seen at the fairs and worked admirably!'

HOW SHERLOCK HOLMES DISCOVERED LITTLE CHARLIE!

While a number of people in the entertainment world have variously claimed to have been responsible for putting young Charlie Chaplin on the road to fame and fortune, the star himself once most firmly attributed the credit to Sherlock Holmes! Or to be more precise, the veteran London actor playing Holmes who gave Charlie his first stage role in 1903.

While he was being interviewed in Hollywood in July 1916 – almost 13 years to the day after his debut in London – Charlie told magazine writer, Charles Lapworth, 'People always connect me and my work with my training under Fred Karno, the vaudeville manager. But as a matter of fact, I owe more to the tutelage of a Mr Saintsbury who gave me my first legitimate engagement as Billy, the boy in Sherlock Holmes, than to anybody in the world.'

H.A. Saintsbury – his Christian names are not given in any theatrical reference book – was one of the stalwarts of the London acting profession, and his gamble in casting a small boy who said he was 14 when he was actually only twelve-and-a-half years old and whose sole previous experience was with a clog dancing troupe, The Eight Lancashire Lads, into what was undeniably an important role, shows remarkable instinct. He deserves, I believe, a little more research than most other Chaplin biographers have given him.

Charlie, in his autobiography, deals more with the play Sherlock Holmes itself than with his mentor, though he does provide us with this nice word picture:

'Mr H.A. Saintsbury, who played Holmes on tour,' he writes, 'was a living replica of the illustrations in the *Strand* Magazine. He had a sensitive face and an inspired forehead. Of all those who played Holmes he was considered the best, even better than William Gillette, the original Holmes and author of the play.'

Saintsbury was born in Chelsea on December 18, 1869, and first worked as a clerk in the Bank of England before following his inclination for the stage and making his debut at the Opera Comique Theatre in March 1887 in Kate Vaughan's revival of *Masks and Faces*.

His first leading role was as the domineering Captain Temple in *Human Nature*, and this was followed by a tour of South Africa in 1893-4 where his company performed a total of 20 plays. In 1897 he formed his own management and thereafter played a variety of

'H.A. Saintsbury was a living replica of the illustrations in the Strand Magazine' – a typical picture of Sherlock Holmes in dramatic action drawn by Sydney Paget.

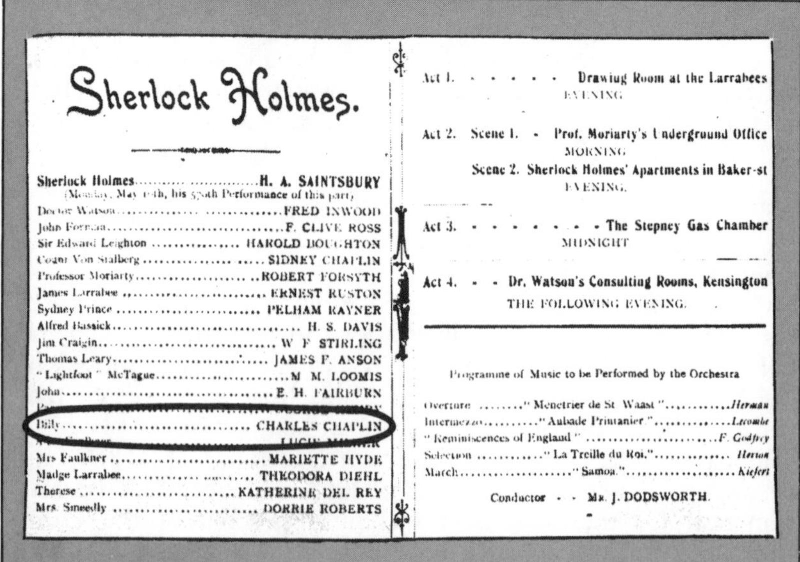

Sherlock Holmes.

Sherlock Holmes.............................H. A. SAINTSBURY
(Monday, May [illegible], his [illegible] Performance of this part)
Doctor Watson.............................FRED INWOOD
John Forman.............................F. CLIVE ROSS
Sir Edward Leighton.............................HAROLD BOUGHTON
Count Von Stalberg.............................SIDNEY CHAPLIN
Professor Moriarty.............................ROBERT FORSYTH
James Larrabee.............................ERNEST RUSTON
Sydney Prince.............................PELHAM RAYNER
Alfred Bassick.............................H. S. DAVIS
Jim Craigin.............................W. F. STIRLING
Thomas Leary.............................JAMES F. ANSON
"Lightfoot" McTague.............................M. M. LOOMIS
John.............................E. H. FAIRBURN
[illegible]
Billy.............................CHARLES CHAPLIN
[illegible]
Mrs Faulkner.............................MARIETTE HYDE
Madge Larrabee.............................THEODORA DIEHL
Therese.............................KATHERINE DEL REY
Mrs. Smeedly.............................DORRIE ROBERTS

Act 1. - - - - - - Drawing Room at the Larrabees
EVENING

Act 2. Scene 1. - Prof. Moriarty's Underground Office
MORNING
Scene 2. Sherlock Holmes' Apartments in Baker-st
EVENING.

Act 3. - - - - - - - The Stepney Gas Chamber
MIDNIGHT

Act 4. - - Dr. Watson's Consulting Rooms, Kensington
THE FOLLOWING EVENING.

Programme of Music to be Performed by the Orchestra

Overture ...."Menetrier de St. Waast"............*Herman*
Intermezzo..........."Aubade Printanier"...............*Lecombe*
"Reminiscences of England"..........................*F. Godfrey*
Selection............"La Treille du Roi."..............*Herton*
March......................"Samoa."......................*Kiefert*

Conductor - - Mr. J. DODSWORTH.

Rare photograph of the young Charlie as Billy, the newspaper boy in H.A. Saintsbury's *Sherlock Holmes*.

major roles such as Hamlet, Shylock, Malvolio and Fagin in *Oliver Twist*. Saintsbury's own favourite leading role was as Charles IX in *King of the Hugenots*.

As well as a performer, he proved himself a skillful dramatist, writing several plays for the stage including a spectacular version of Dumas' *The Three Musketeers* and a drama, *The Four Just Men*. (Chaplin himself was later to write a comedy sketch inspired by this, 'The Twelve Just Men'!)

But it was for his performances as the Great Detective that Saintsbury became a leading name with the public. In all he played Holmes 1,404 times in two productions: *Sherlock Holmes*, which he began in 1902, and later *The Speckled Band* which opened at the Adelphi Theatre in 1910.

In 1916 he became the first English actor to play Holmes on the screen in the Samuelson Film Company's six-reel silent version of *The Valley of Fear* directed by Alexander Butler from a script by Harry Engholm. The part of Dr Watson was played by another stage veteran, Arthur M. Cullin.

When Saintsbury died on June 19, 1939, aged 69, one obituary referred to him quite simply as, 'the original Sherlock Holmes.'

This, then, was the man that the small and nervous young Chaplin went to see at his imposing club, The Green Room, in Leicester Square in June 1903. Chaplin had secured the interview by lying about his age to a theatrical agent who just happened at that moment to be looking for a child actor to play the part of Billy the page boy in the Charles Frohman production of *Sherlock Holmes* which was to begin touring later that month with Saintsbury in the title role. As was customary, the leading actor had the right of veto on the cast.

The actual role of Billy, which the great American actor William Gillette had specially created for his adapaption of the Arthur Conan Doyle stories in 1899, was supposed to be a smart young fellow who introduced clients to Holmes in his study or else ran messages. The colourful role had first been played on the stage in America by a youngster named Henry McArdle busying himself on Gillette/Holmes' behalf. When Charlie secured the role in the English production he was the seventh boy to have donned the trim, buttoned uniform.

Saintsbury was obviously taken with the dark-haired youngster, though he thought him so small he asked several other members of the cast to take a look at him! Nonetheless, the overjoyed Chaplin was signed on as a member of the company at the princely sum of two pounds ten shillings per week!

Interestingly, Chaplin briefly played another role with his benefactor before appearing as Billy. Saintsbury had just written a four-act play called, *Jim: A Romance of Cockayne*, which contained the role of a newspaper boy named Sammy. For two weeks, first at Kingston-on-Thames and then in Fulham, he worked hard at the part, learning everything he could from his mentor. By the time Sherlock Holmes went into rehearsal, he was feeling increasingly confident about the profession he had chosen, as he later revealed.

'Those first rehearsals were a revelation,' he said. 'They opened up a new world of technique. I had no idea that there was such a thing as stage-craft, timing, pausing, a cue to turn, to sit, but it came naturally to me. Only one fault Mr Saintsbury corrected: I moved my head and 'mugged' too much when I talked. After

Duke of York's Theatre

ST MARTIN'S LANE WC

Proprietors ... ... Mr & Mrs Frank Wyatt
Sole Lessee and Manager ... ... CHARLES FROHMAN

CHARLES FROHMAN PRESENTS
A DRAMA IN FOUR ACTS
BY A. CONAN DOYLE
AND WILLIAM GILLETTE
ENTITLED

SHERLOCK HOLMES

BEING A HITHERTO UNPUBLISHED EPISODE
IN THE CAREER OF THE GREAT DETECTIVE
AND SHOWING HIS CONNECTION WITH THE

STRANGE CASE OF MISS FAULKNER

CHARACTERS IN THE PLAY	COMPANY APPEARING IN THE CAST
SHERLOCK HOLMES	WILLIAM GILLETTE
DOCTOR WATSON	KENNETH RIVINGTON
JOHN FORMAN	EUGENE MAYEUR
SIR EDWARD LEIGHTON	REGINALD DANCE
COUNT VON STAHLBURG	FREDERICK MORRIS
PROFESSOR MORIARTY	GEORGE SUMNER
JAMES LARRABEE	FRANCIS CARLYLE
SIDNEY PRINCE	QUINTON McPHERSON
ALFRED BASSICK	WILLIAM H. DAY
JIM CRAIGIN	CHRIS WALKER
THOMAS LEARY	HENRY WALTERS
"LIGHTFOOT" MCTAGUE	WALTER DISON
JOHN	THOMAS QUINTON
PARSONS	G. MERTON
BILLY	CHARLES CHAPLIN
ALICE FAULKNER	MARIE DORO
MRS. FAULKNER	DE OLIA WEBSTER
MADGE LARRABEE	ADELAIDE PRINCE
THERESE	SYBIL CAMPBELL
MRS. SMEEDLEY	ETHEL LORRIMORE

THE PLACE IS LONDON
THE TIME TEN YEARS AGO

FIRST ACT—DRAWING ROOM AT THE LARRABEES'—EVENING
SECOND ACT—Scene I—PROFESSOR MORIARTY'S UNDERGROUND OFFICE—MORNING
Scene II—SHERLOCK HOLMES' APARTMENTS IN BAKER STREET—EVENING
THIRD ACT—THE STEPNEY GAS CHAMBER—MIDNIGHT
FOURTH ACT—DOCTOR WATSON'S CONSULTING ROOM KENSINGTON—THE FOLLOWING EVENING

Scenery by Ernest Gros — Incidental Music by William Furst

INTERMISSIONS
Between the 1st and 2nd Acts, 9 minutes
Between the 2nd and 3rd Acts, 7 minutes
Between the 3rd and 4th Acts, 8 minutes

MATINEE every Saturday at 2.15 o'clock

BUSINESS MANAGER—JAMES W MATHEWS — ACTING MANAGER—ROBERT M EBERLE
STAGE MANAGER—WILLIAM POSTANCE — MUSICAL DIRECTOR—JOHN CROOK

ICES TEA AND COFFEE can be had of the Attendants

rehearsing a few scenes he was astonished and wanted to know if I had acted before. What a glow of satisfaction, pleasing Mr Saintsbury and the rest of the cast!'

Sherlock Holmes, with its sub-title, '*The Strange Case of Miss Faulkner*', opened at the Pavilion Theatre in east London on July 2, 1903. Although the production had already been staged before with Saintsbury and well reviewed, it still attracted some new notices and among these was one from *The Stage* which must undoubtedly have pleased the youngest member of the cast.

'A faithful portrait of Billy is given by Master Charles Chaplin,' it ran, 'who shows considerable ability, and bids fair to develop into a capable and clever actor.'

Another reference to Charlie's stage debut published some years afterwards in *Passing Show* magazine, however, managed to confuse the productions of Jim and Sherlock Holmes to produce a classic newspaper gaff. Talking about this early stage work, the paper said: 'We heard of him first as a newsboy in a one act Sherlock Holmes play entitled *A Romance of Cocaine*.' If he ever

William Gillette, the American actor who had brought Sherlock Holmes to the stage, and with whom Charlie Chaplin appeared in 1905, as the showbill reproduced here shows.

saw the story, how Charlie must have chuckled!

After a week in London, Saintsbury, Chaplin and Co set off on a 45-week tour through the South of England, on to the Midlands and finally into the North and Scotland. Over 500 performances were given, the half-century mark being recorded in Dewsbury where the audience were each presented with Souvenir Programmes printed in red and blue, a rare item in those days.

The tour finished in London in July 1904 and Charlie, now a rather self-assured page, was fêted by one review in an evening newspaper: 'The boy Billy is acted with rare ability by Master Charles Chaplin.'

Strangely, though Saintsbury set off on another tour of Sherlock Holmes just one month later, Charlie was not signed to continue as Billy. It was, in fact, to mark the parting of the ways for Chaplin from the man who had given him his start in the world of entertainment. One can only guess at any emotion either might have felt as this moment of time, but Charlie certainly never forgot his gratitude to the older thespian.

For the boy actor there followed a four month period of 'resting' – to use that delightful actors' euphemism – until another of Charles Frohman's companies based in the Midlands offered him the chance to reprise the role in a production starring Kenneth Rivington as the Great Detective. Charlie evidently spent an arduous four months on the road with this production, and a sign that he was perhaps growing a little restless can be judged from one review which noted, 'Mr Charles Chaplin as Billy is good, but overdoes the part a little.'

The latent comic in the boy – still not yet 15 – was obviously beginning to stir.

In September 1905, William Gillette, the originator of Holmes on the stage, came to London to mount a new play, *Clarissa*, complete with a one-act drama as a curtain raiser called *The Painful Predicament of Sherlock Holmes*. Billy the page boy was featured once again and Charlie happily accepted this new version of the role because it offered him his first chance of appearing in the West End – at the prestigious Duke of York's Theatre!

Unhappily, *Clarissa* proved a disaster, and along with its closing after just 13 performances went Charlie's role in the curtain-raiser. Gillette, though, quickly recovered his sang-froid and agreed to appear in his own version of *Sherlock Holmes*. This proved an instant success: Gillette being wildly applauded for his performance as the Great Detective. Charlie, who was conveniently to hand and fully experienced as Billy, was happy to stay in work and likewise earned good notices for his playing of the faithful page. The show drew packed houses until just before Christmas when other engagements took Gillette back across the Atlantic.

It is a not widely known fact that Gillette and Chaplin were destined to meet again in very different circumstances, though Sherlock Holmes was once again the magnet that brought them together. In March 1916, when Charlie was firmly established in Hollywood and busy making movies for the Essanay Company, Gillette was signed by the same people to film his play for the cinema in seven parts using members of his own company and a number of the Essanay players. Appearing with Gillette were Edward Fielding as Dr Watson and Ernest Maupain as the infamous Professor Moriarty.

A legend that was repeated to me in Hollywood has it that Chaplin and Gillette met again on the set of Sherlock Holmes and happily talked about their times together in London. And, says the story, the veteran actor asked his 'faithful page' if he would care to make a guest appearance in the photoplay of the story with which, of course, he was so familiar. No evidence exists as to Chaplin's reply, and even the most careful scrutiny of the silent movie has failed to reveal anyone who bears the slightest resemblance to Chaplin! (By a curious twist of fate, Charlie was at that time filming *Police* in which he played an escaped convict on the run from the law!)

However, to return to the story of Chaplin and Sherlock Holmes, no sooner had the Gillette show closed at the end of 1905, than Charlie was sought out again to play Billy in another production being staged by a Blackburn theatre proprietor named

Harry Yorke who had secured the rights from the Frohman company. For nine weeks more he busied himself in the service of a new Holmes played by one H. Lawrence Leyton.

On March 3, 1906 he took what was to prove his very last bow as Billy at the Theatre Royal in Rochdale. Immediately afterwards he inserted an advertisement in *The Stage* announcing that he was available for new engagements. (This modest piece of early Chaplin memorabilia is reproduced in these pages.) It had been a hard and demanding apprenticeship with *Sherlock Holmes*, and undoubtedly Chaplin had learned a great deal from H.A. Saintsbury – and William Gillette to a lesser degree – which was to be of enormous value to him when he began to give full vent to his latent comic talent, first on the stage with Fred Karno and his company whom he joined in 1907, and later in films.

I am reminded that one of H.A. Saintsbury's remarks to his young page during the course of *Sherlock Holmes* was an emphatic, 'Billy, you're a smart boy!' By merely changing the name Billy to Charlie it might equally be said to have been even more apposite in real life!

MASTER CHARLES CHAPLIN,
Sherlock Holmes Co.
Disengaged March 5th.
Coms., 9, Tavistock Place. Tele., 2,187 Hop.

Charlie's announcement in *The Stage*, March 1, 1906, that he is ready for new horizons...

ON THE ROAD TO FAME

It was in the year 1903 that Charlie really set out on the road to stardom when he fortuitously landed the job with the Charles Frohman Touring Company, first to play in the short-lived drama, *Jim, A Romance of Cockayne* and then appearing as Billy in the adaptation of *Sherlock Holmes* with H.A. Saintsbury. The company's wardrobe mistress and occasional actress, Edith Scales, remembered the young thespian's first days on the road during an interview she gave at her home in Scarborough, Yorkshire in May 1931:

'I first met Charlie when he joined the road company which was touring England with Charles Frohman's *Sherlock Holmes*. There was no one to look after the boy, so I took him under my wing.

'Charlie was all right when we were in London because he felt at home, but when we started touring he needed keeping an eye on. I remember one Saturday that Charlie was late for a matinee performance in which he was playing two parts, that of Billy, a newsboy detective, and a page boy.

'When he finally arrived at the theatre and found that another boy was dressed in his clothes and on stage, he broke out in tears and could not be comforted until the beginning of the second act, when he was allowed to resume his two roles.

'Even at the age of 15 (he was actually 14), Charlie was a hard-headed business man. To make extra money on the road he bought a five shilling camera and, during his free time, used to go about, usually among groups of working people, snapping their pictures.

'He then printed the photographs himself and sold them to his customers for threepence and sixpence each. He was not afraid to work hard, and he looked upon no honest way of making money as beneath his dignity, even though he enjoyed the status and had the temperament of an actor.

'One day when the company was staying at the Market Hotel in Blackburn, Charlie noticed that the hotel sitting room was filled with farmers in town because it was market day. He walked into the midst of the country folks and began singing songs in what was then his pronounced Cockney accent. And he finished his bit of entertainment by going into a clog-dance.

'His audience laughed until the tears streamed down their faces,

Photograph of Charlie as the page in H.A. Saintsbury's *Sherlock Holmes*.

but their amusement was somewhat lessened when Charlie circulated among them with his hat in his hand. He intended that his audience should pay for the impromptu show – and they did!

'Charlie wasn't mean, but he never threw away money unnecessarily. I recall how he used to check every item on the bills rendered him by landladies when we were on the road, and how he used to knock off items for service he hadn't been given. If he had been out to tea one day during the week, he would deduct a proportionate amount from the bill.

'Everybody liked Charlie, though, he was a wonderfully clever boy. He deserved all the fame that later came to him.'

ONE OF FRED KARNO'S ARMY!

After leaving the Post Office and working for several years as a ships steward and bandsman, Charlie's older brother, Sydney, also decided to try his luck on the stage, and in July 1906 joined Fred Karno's famous touring burlesque company, rapidly becoming a star and appearing in America. In 1908, Sydney got his kid brother an audition with the great music hall performer turned showman and manager, and this was recalled by Mr T. Scott Bell, Karno's secretary for many years, in an interview he gave in London in August 1915:

'Charlie was introduced to us by his elder brother, Syd, who was at that time the leading man in our town troupe. Mr Karno agreed to give him a chance. One of the earliest shows he played in was 'The Football Match' at the London Coliseum, where he showed great promise.

'In those days Mr Karno made a speciality of pantomime sketches, as he believed that actions often speak louder than words. He quickly perceived that Charlie was more eloquent with his hands than most people are with their vocal organs.

'Charlie took part in one after another of our companies, thus getting a first rate schooling. He always showed himself a good, reliable performer.

The great showman, Fred Karno (centre, front row) with just one of his famous touring companies. Charlie is standing, partly obscured, beneath the chandelier in the very back row! Alfred Reeves, who became Charlie's Hollywood manager, is third from the left on the front row.

Grand Christmas Production

Of FRED KARNO'S latest Burlesque

"THE FOOTBALL MATCH."

Over 100 Auxiliaries. **Catchy Music.**

Clever Comedians. **Wonderful Scenery.**

Realistic Football Match—in the rain—with real Football Champions contesting, and the usual High-class Variety Entertainment.

Special Matinees Xmas Week—See future announcements.

TWICE NIGHTLY.

Fred Karno and (left) an advertisement for 'The Football Match' in which Charlie made his comedy debut.

ydney Chaplin, Charlie's older rother, who introduced him to ed Karno. Sydney himself later ecame a well-known film actor.

'We always thought him more than a little eccentric, however. He was very untidy in his person. Even when he was leading man, he would often turn up at train-call in a pair of old carpet slippers, his collar only partly buttoned, and his tie hanging loose round his neck! I remember he went to Paris like that!

'At last we decided to send him on tour in America. The repertoire included three sketches, into which Charlie had put a good deal of his amusing personality – though, mind you, the business in all of them was of Mr Karno's own creating.

'The most popular of the three was 'The Mumming Birds', Charlie playing the part of a drunken swell. Another of the sketches was 'The Wow-Wows', a skit on secret societies. Charlie was initiated into the Secret Society of the Wow-Wows. You can imagine the farcical nature of the business.

'The third piece was 'The Smoking Concert' in which various people were called upon to entertain and the proceedings were interupted by an ineberiated Charlie.

'The company went all round the Sullivan & Considine circuit twice, visiting all the principal cities east and west, including Salt Lake City, and travelling as far north as Winnipeg and south as far as New Orleans.

'It was while Charlie was in Kansas City that the offers for cinema work became too tempting for him to resist, and he left us, joining the Keystone Film Company in Los Angeles. A year later, the Essanay Company secured his services.

'We have no official information, but we understand the Essanay people are paying him three hundred pounds a week, plus a royalty on the films he plays in, which is estimated to bring his income up to five hundred pounds a week.

'So you can see the stories that we let him go are untrue. It was the other way about. Had he returned, on the completion of his contract, we should have given him the leading role in one or other of our most popular sketches.

'But, of course, the inducements offered by the film companies would have prevailed sooner or later. Few men can stand out against big money, and Charlie is only about 30 years of age now.

'Charlie is the greatest film-actor of the day, outclassing the late John Bunny as the artist outranks the photographer. Bunny's face was his fortune; Charlie has won his way by sheer merit. He is an artist in mirth, and can put more fun into a simple gesture or pose than any man living.

'That's why the cinema people collared him!'

Charlie himself paid tribute to Fred Karno's part in his development as a comedian in a special interview he gave to *Variety* in January 1942, a few months after the showman's death, aged 75. Interestingly, he strongly contradicts Mr Scott Bell's description of his appearance!

'At that time I told people I had been in show business all my life. Even when I was in my teens I looked about six years old and talked like a little old man. I used to wear a bowler with an air, a paddock coat and a cane that I thought lent a dash of suavity. I believed I was just the cheese!

Billy Ritchie who worked with Chaplin for Fred Karno and later became famous for his impersonations of the Little Tramp.

'Syd thought I was the greatest actor in the world. Karno got sick finally of hearing about Syd's brother. Syd wanted to leave the company and asked that I be given a chance. In order to save expenses Karno finally agreed and gave me a try in 'The Football Match.'

'The part was that of the comic villain who tries to bribe the goalkeeper. I was just there to feed the comedian, but I didn't know that at first. When I found out I put in some new business. The show opened at the Coliseum in London – and after the third night they started to applaud my entrances.

'I came on stage with my back to the audience. I was wearing a frock coat and a great false nose. I went through all of the clichés

of the villain and then turned round slowly, with all of the unction in the world. I tangled my finger in my watch chain and I used a cane to good advantage.

'I never got rid of the cane!

'Fred Karno was undoubtedly the greatest mime in show business at the turn of the century. He streamlined the traditional conventional pantomime, like that of the Drury Lane Theatre, and made it intelligible to the world audience.

'He was an acrobat in the beginning and first appeared with his brothers as the Karno Trio. Between gymnastic stunts he invented business and soon sensed that audiences were more amused by his mimicry than the spectacular performances. He was also the first to synchronise pantomime with music.

'At one time he had between 18 and 20 companies touring all over England and many parts of the world such as America, South America and Africa. No language was necessary, because the acting of the troupe was vivid and expressive enough to bring laughter from any race.

'All of the pieces we did, as I remember them, were cruel and boisterous, filled with acrobatic humour and low, knockabout comedy. Each man working for Karno had to have perfect timing and had to know the peculiarities of every one else in the cast so that we could, collectively, achieve a tempo.

'It took about a year for an actor to get the repertoire of a dozen shows down pat. Karno required us to know a number of parts so that players could be interchanged. When one left the company it was like taking a screw or a pin out of a very delicate piece of machinery.

'I am sure that my work with Karno schooled me in the technique of pantomime and gave me the basis for my motion picture work.

'I reckon that Karno made about $1,000,000 out of his mass production of pantomime. He also developed some fine comedians like Harry Weldon, who was Stiffy the goalkeeper in my first sketch; Billy Reeves, the brother of my general manager, Alfred Reeves; Billy Ritchie who was the first drunk in 'The Mumming Birds' and, of course, Stan Laurel.'

(It is interesting that Chaplin mentions Billy Ritchie here as he was briefly famous for his impersonations of the Little Tramp on film – complete with derby hat, moustache and cane – in pictures such as *Partners in Crime* (1914) and *A Meeting for Cheating* (1915). He certainly gets no mention in Chaplin's *Autobiography* and it was probably due to the two mens' friendship from the Karno days that spared Ritchie from the litigation which Charlie brought against others who tried to imitate his success on the screen. Billy died bizarrely in 1921 from injuries inflicted during a badly timed film stunt with an ostrich!)

'WAGGER'S' FILM DEBUT

One of the stars of Fred Karno's company when Charlie joined was Fred Kitchen, a burly comic, who had first appeared on the stage as a baby in arms and developed into a master of comedy and mime, famous for his catch-phrase, 'Meredith, we're in!' from his sketch about a bailiff. He actually had this expression engraved on his tombstone when he died in 1957! Even before the young man destined for super-stardom joined the troupe, Kitchen was using a series of walks, kicks and falls in his act which Charlie was later to adopt. A few years before his death, living in retirement in Hampton Hill, Middlesex, Fred talked about the young comedian he had encouraged as well as revealing some interesting facts about the very first film in which Chaplin appeared.

Charlie's impromptu appearance before the newsreel camera in Jersey in 1912 was very similar to that he made in his second Keystone movie, *Kid Auto Races at Venice* (1914).

'When young Charlie Chaplin joined us he was given the nickname 'Wagger' after the Cockney term 'Charlie Wag' for anyone who is a bit of a comedian. I took a liking to the skinny young lad right away and I could sense he had talent.

'So I took him under my wing and taught him the rudiments of being a funny man by under- rather than over-playing.

'I was actually the first comedian to wear oversize boots. Fred Karno came up with this idea to make a bit of business out of my shambling stage walk which was half way between a shuffle and a hop. I had to smile when Charlie later started to wear a pair of large boots himself.

'I also taught him my 'ashtray' kick – throwing a cigarette over my shoulder and kicking it away with my heel before it hit the ground.

'Many years later when Charlie had become a star in Hollywood, a friend asked me why I didn't visit America. "Why should I?" I replied, "if I went there everyone would say I was imitating Charlie!"

'I don't think many people know that Charlie actually first appeared on film *before* he left Britain. It happened in August 1912 when we were on tour with 'Mumming Birds' in Jersey, one of the Channel Islands. We were playing the St Helier Opera House.

'It was the time of the famous Jersey Carnival of Flowers, and a film cameraman had been sent down to film the procession for the cinema newsreels. After some difficulty in setting up his camera, the man managed to get it in a good spot on the racecourse, and with his eye glued to the 'finder' started cranking the handle at the moment a particularly fine floral float came into his line of vision.

'Suddenly, he was roused from his preoccupation by a yell of delight from the crowd. A slender little man had emerged unobserved from somewhere and had been entertaining them for some minutes by performing a variety of curious shambling steps just in front of the camera.

'A particularly funny bit of business had broken the silence and the on-lookers had given him a round of applause. It was then that the cameraman discovered his machine had taken several dozen feet of the procession as well as the comic performance by the little man.

'That man was, of course, Charlie Chaplin!

'Charlie later told me that the thing he remembered best about the incident was the voice of a little boy protesting afterwards, "Oh, mummy, why has the funny man gone away?"

'Charlie said it did his confidence no end of good – and it seems now like a kind of omen, doesn't it?'

(Despite the most extensive research, this piece of film of Chaplin's screen debut captured by the *Topical Gazette* has not yet come to light.)

A RIDE TO A FALL!

Among the other artists who toured with Charlie in the Fred Karno troupe was an attractive young singer and dancer called Winifred Morris. In September 1964, after Chaplin's autobiography had been published, she wrote from her home in Wokingham, Berkshire, recalling a piece of real-life slapstick which occurred while the company was on the road.

'I was on tour with Charlie Chaplin in Fred Karno's Company, and his autobiography has brought back many happy memories for me. One incident could have been part of a Chaplin film.

'While we were touring though Devon, he decided to ride on the top of the bus where all our boxes, cases, etc, were strapped. He was the "top comic" and was warned not to take any risks as we had no understudies.

'But up he went and was soon acting to the clouds reciting those famous lines from Dickens' *A Tale of Two Cities*: "It is a far, far better thing that I do, than I have ever . . ."

'At that very moment an overhanging branch caught him and bowled him over! He was then ordered to ride inside the bus and stop acting the goat outside.

'On another occasion we were playing the Hippodrome, Manchester, and George Robey was starring at the Palace opposite. One evening between the two houses a knock came on my dressing room door, the dresser went to answer it, and came back saying, "Mr George Robey wants to speak to you."

'I went to the door and when I asked, "What is it you want, Mr Robey?" there was silence.

'Then a large pair of eyes widened and that inimitable quirk of the mouth – I knew then who it was: Charles. He was dressed up and going round our dressing rooms, trying to fool us!

'He was a true artiste in more ways than one. The greatest comic England ever had.'

An early cartoon of Charlie by a renowned spotter of future stars, the artist Allan Morley.

THE TALENT OF JIMMY THE FEARLESS

Alfred Reeves was the son of a lion tamer who grew up in the world of the circus until he became a tour manager for Fred Karno, running his American shows from 1905 onwards. In 1910 he was responsible for selecting Charlie to lead a troupe to America, and in the following interview which he gave in Hollywood in August 1934 describes how this came about. Charlie was deeply appreciative of what Alfred Reeves had done for him and in 1918 invited him to cross the Atlantic and become his manager.

'It was a pretty young soubrette called Amy Minister who was appearing in one of Fred Karno's troupes who first told me about Charlie Chaplin. The year was 1910 and I was in London looking for new players to go to America.

'"Al, there's a clever boy in the Karno troupe at the Holloway Empire," she told me. "His name's Charlie Chaplin. He's a wonderful kid and a marvellous actor." I told her I would have a look at him and a couple of days later went off down to Holloway.

'Now you'll hardly believe it, but just as I popped into the theatre there was this young actor Amy had spoken about putting great dramatic fire into that good old speech, "Another shot rang out, and another redskin bit the dust." The part he was playing was that of a dime-novel-struck London errand boy forever reading Wild West blood-and-thunder thrillers!

'And that's not all that was different about the Charlie we know. He didn't even *look* the same.

'He looked the typical London street urchin who knows every inch of the town as he darts through hurrying throngs and dodges in and out of rushing traffic, managing by some miracle to escape with his life. He had a cap on the back of his head and wore a shabby old suit, short in the sleeves and frayed at the cuffs – a suit he had long since outgrown.

'The piece was called 'Jimmy the Fearless' and Charlie had the leading part, even though he was only in his teens. But it was not until he did something strikingly characteristic that I realised he was a rare find.

'His father in the skit was ordering him to drop his novel and eat his supper – "Get on with it now, m'lad!" – and jabbing a loaf of bread at him. Charlie, I noticed, cut the bread without once taking his eyes off his book.

'But what particularly attracted my attention was that while he absentmindedly kept cutting the bread, he held the knife in his left hand. Charlie's left-handed, but I didn't know it then. The next thing I knew, he had carved that loaf into the shape of a concertina!

'After the performance I went to his dressing room and asked Charlie if he would go to America. "Only too gladly, if you'll give me the chance," he cried. I told him I'd have a talk with Karno.

'On hearing this, he wiped the smudge of make-up off his face to give his smile full play, and I saw he was a very good-looking boy. I had made up my mind about him before leaving his dressing room.

'"Well," considered Karno when I told him what I had in mind, "you can have him for the American company if you think he's old enough for the parts." We were then giving 'A Night in an English Music Hall', 'A Night in a London Club' and 'A Night in a Secret Society'.

'"He's old enough," I told Karno, "and big enough and clever enough for anything."

'That settled it – and I lost no time in carrying the news to Amy Minister. "You're a good judge of talent, my girl," I assured her. "What about a bit of dinner together?" A little celebration was in order, for, thanks to her, Charlie Chaplin had been "discovered" for America.

'And my good fortune didn't end there. For I'd also discovered the young lady who later became Mrs Alfred Reeves!'

'A dime novel struck London boy' – and the kind of publications Chaplin liked: the detective stories of Nick Carter!

THE LAND OF FUN AND OPPORTUNITY

Charlie Chaplin was not the only young actor on the Karno tour of America who was destined for world-wide fame – the comic Stan Laurel was also to secure his own place in the cinema hall of fame when he linked up with Oliver Hardy in 1926 to create one of the immortal screen partnerships. In September 1929, Laurel gave a revealing interview in Hollywood while the pair were making their first talkie, *Unaccustomed As We Are*, in which he described how he and Charlie docked in New York in 1910 and what life had in store for them in the months which followed.

'It was a September day when we first saw the American shore line. We were all on deck straining our eyes to get a first glimpse of the country. Charlie was just as nervous as the rest of us, although he tried to cover it up with a show of unconcern.

'Just as we saw land, the sun came out for a few minutes. Charlie put his foot up on the rail of the boat, swung his arm landward in one of his usual burlesque, dramatic gestures, and declared, "America, I have come to conquer!"

'We had to reach New York on a certain day to fill our engagement, and, as there was no regular steamer arriving there in time,

On the high seas to America: Chaplin (with his head through the life preserver) and Stan Laurel (far left) on board the *Cairnrona Castle* in 1910 with other members of the Fred Karno troupe bound for New York.

Stan Laurel, Charlie's stage colleague, who also later became famous in Hollywood as half of the Laurel and Hardy duo.

we engaged passages on a cattle boat! All the way over we rehearsed the new act with which we hoped to make our first American hit. We called it, 'A Night in an English Secret Society' and we thought it was funnier than anything we had ever done.

'But, oh, what a flop it was! It fell flatter than flat when we played it for the first time at the Colonial Theatre in New York. So after eleven performances we returned to our old, sure-fire piece, 'A Night in an English Music Hall' – known in England as 'Mumming Birds'.

'Charlie was the featured comedian in the troupe, while I was billed as second in importance and his understudy. He was earning twelve pounds a week, while I was only getting five – a mere pittance, in view of American living costs – but we had fun in those days, with Charlie always the life and soul of the party.

'Charlie and I lived together, sharing the same room, for more than two years, and many's the time we've cooked our dinners in our room. I fried the chops, while Charlie sat close to the door

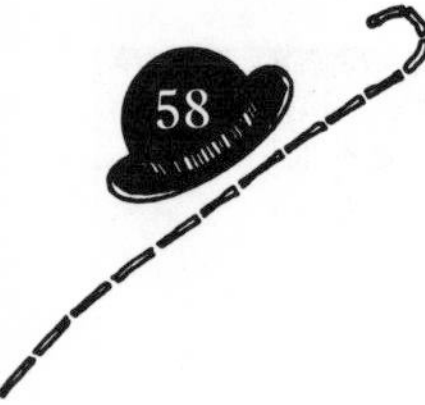

playing his mandolin to keep the landlady from hearing the sizzling of the meat over the gas – which was put there for lighting purposes only and not with any idea of cooking!

'Charlie was the ringleader in everything. Even then we all felt there was something in him which was different from other men. We didn't know what it was; we couldn't put our fingers on it; but it *was* there. He was always trying to do queer and unusual things.

'I remember the day he decided to learn to play the 'cello. He knew nothing about the instrument, but he bought a second-hand one and lugged it home to our room in the hotel. After the matinee he did not join the party for dinner. When it was time to go back to the theatre for the evening performance and he had not yet shown up at our favourite restaurant, I went over to the hotel to look for him.

'I opened the door of the bedroom and, coming from behind the closed door of the bathroom, I heard terrible whines and moans and scrapings. Then I found him with his 'cello, posing in front of the full-length mirror in the bathroom. He had tousled his hair into a mass of curls. With grandiose gestures he was pulling the bow back and forth across the strings while he admired his reflected self!

'His imitation of one of these high-brow artists of the concert stage was so ridiculously funny that I simply stood there and howled. Finally, we realised that it was time for the show, 'cello or no 'cello. The next day he forgot all about his musical career and turned to something else.

'Another time he went crazy over Calabash pipes. Someone came round with a beautiful coloured pipe. Immediately Charlie decided to have one like it, so out he went to the nearest tobacco shop and came back with a handsome, white pipe. He was always terribly impatient and nervously active. Nothing annoyed him so much as delay of any kind. That pipe had to glow immediately.

'He smoked morning, noon and night. The first thing he did when he got out of bed in the morning was to fill and light that pipe. He went to bed at night with the darned thing in his mouth, but then one day the pipe refused to glow as fast as he thought it should.

'In a moment of disgust he threw it out of the window as far as he could hurl it, and dragged out a package of his neglected cigarettes. His pipe smoking days were gone for ever!

'Charlie had a terrible habit of always sauntering in at the last minute just before we were due to go on stage. I suffered many pangs of uncertainty because of this as it was my job to go on in his place if he was not there.

'But I never had the chance to take his place in all the years we played together, although many times I was dressed and ready. He always showed up just in the nick of time, smiling and unperturbed. His mind was usually a thousand miles away, dwelling in some land where the rest of us poor troupers could not follow.

'Then came the day when Charlie listened to the lure of the movies. We all prophesied, blindly, that he was making a great mistake, that he should remain true to the stage. But he passed off his departure with his usual clowning, and made a grand gesture of farewell. Still, there was a tremble in his handclasp. After all, we had been trouping together for more than seven years. We all wished him well from the very bottom of our hearts, but we secretly congratulated ourselves on possessing a superior wisdom.

'I took Charlie's place, but it was a poor substitute for the one and only Chaplin. The show went on for several months, but when Charlie left us the old spirit seemed to leave with him. The heart of the act was gone. Then, for the first time, the rest of us fully realised the power of the genius that is Chaplin's.

'When the tour came to an end I decided to stay and try my luck in American vaudeville and variety shows. Despite the success that Charlie was having in the movies, I was afraid to try them myself.

'If the words "Limitation is the sincerest form of flattery" are true, then I surely proved to Charlie the depth of my admiration in my vaudeville take-offs of his clowning pantomime. Since I had played with him for so long, and since, as his understudy, I had learned to copy every trick of his movements and speech, I followed in the wake of his sensational popularity by imitating him for the entertainment of the two-a-day audiences. Even Charlie admitted that I made a pretty good job of it. I should have, after seven years of study, shouldn't I?

'Then one day in 1917 I ran into Charlie in the street when I was playing one of the Los Angeles theatres. I had just been offered a job in films by the Universal Company and I couldn't make up my mind what to do.

'It was a curious trick of fate that we should have met then – almost seven years to the day when Charlie had made that joking prophecy on the boat about his future fame which had come so miraculously true. He at once urged me to come into the movie field, foreseeing, prophet-like once again, its increasing possibilities.

'This time I knew he was right – and I was happy to follow him through the studio gates into what became a new and even more successful phase of my life.'

Charlie drew this sketch of Stan Laurel late in 1912, and with heavy emphasis on the drunk sketch they both appeared in wrote underneath: 'Well, Stan! May your path be a Rosy One!! From Your Old Pal, Chas. Chaplin, Fred Karno Co., Seattle, Washington, USA, December 28, 1912'.

CHARLIE THE KEYSTONE KOP?

Mack Sennett who put Charlie on the road to film stardom.

While Charlie was touring America he met another comedian who lady luck was going to shine upon – Groucho Marx, the New York-born master of ad lib who began his career as a boy singer at the age of 11 and later joined with his brothers to form one of the most famous comedy teams in the movies. Like Charlie, Groucho worked for some years on the gruelling vaudeville circuit, and in an interview in 1935 in Hollywood recalled his first meeting with the English comedian. Groucho also makes the interesting statement that during his time with Mack Sennett, Charlie actually appeared as one of the legendary Keystone Cops.

'I was on the Pantages Circuit, the last act on the bill, doing four shows a day. There was a three-hour layover in Winnipeg before jumping to the coast. As a rule, I made a bee-line for the pool room. It was generally warmer!

'This particular night I decided to take in a show. I had a friend playing on the Sullivan-Considine Circuit. Considine was the father of the Metro-Goldwyn-Meyer producer, John W. Considine jnr.

'The audience was roaring with laughter. Then I saw Chaplin for the first time. I had never heard people laugh like that. I began to laugh, too.

'His act was called 'A Night at the Club': it was supposed to be an English social club. Chaplin sat at a table and ate soda crackers one after another. A woman up front was singing all the while, but nobody heard a note. They were intent on Chaplin's every move.

'A fine stream of cracker dust was coming out of his mouth. He kept that up for fifteen minutes. Also on the table was a large basket of oranges. He started to pick up the oranges and throw them at the woman.

'One of the oranges knocked the pianist off his chair. People became hysterical. There never was such laughter. I thought he was the greatest fellow I had ever seen on the stage.

'I was so impressed by Chaplin that I sought him out after the show and we became friends. The two circuits that we were on made the same towns, and when we were on stage at the same times we would visit each other between shows. Finally, we both landed in Los Angeles.

'One day Charlie called me up. He said he had been offered

Charlie's first feature length comedy, *Tillie's Punctured Romance*, co-starring Marie Dressler, which was released by Keystone in November 1914.

Groucho Marx as one of the 'Four Nightingales' vaudeville act in the mid-1910's. He is the top figure above his brothers, Harpo and Gummo, with Leo Levin at the bottom.

$100 a week to go with Keystone. "What's the matter?" I said, "isn't it enough?" Chaplin was then getting about $35 a week. "It's too much, I can't be worth $100 a week!" he replied.

'But he finally accepted the motion picture offer. I went East. Chaplin began to appear with the Keystone Cops and then went into his own movies. When I returned to Los Angeles, he was getting $500 a week. He was very happy!

'It's an amazing world. When I first met Charlie Chaplin we often shot craps together. The stakes were a penny and the fellow who won 50 cents was considered a financier. The loser of such a sum tightened his belt for breakfast. It's a little frightening the way those years have passed!'

Chaplin's alleged appearances in bit part roles as one of the Kops in the famous Keystone comedies remains to this day another of the mysteries of his career. In 1965, almost 50 years later, Charlie told an interviewer that during 1914 he had filled in the odd spare day between making his pictures under Mack Sennett's supervision by playing one of the famous Kops. Because of the easy-going manner in which studios were run at this time, and Charlie's irresistible urge to clown for the cameras, the story sounds believable, though the figure of Chaplin is not easy to identify in any of the Keystone Kops movies. Which is not to say that he is *not* among those madcap figures somewhere . . .

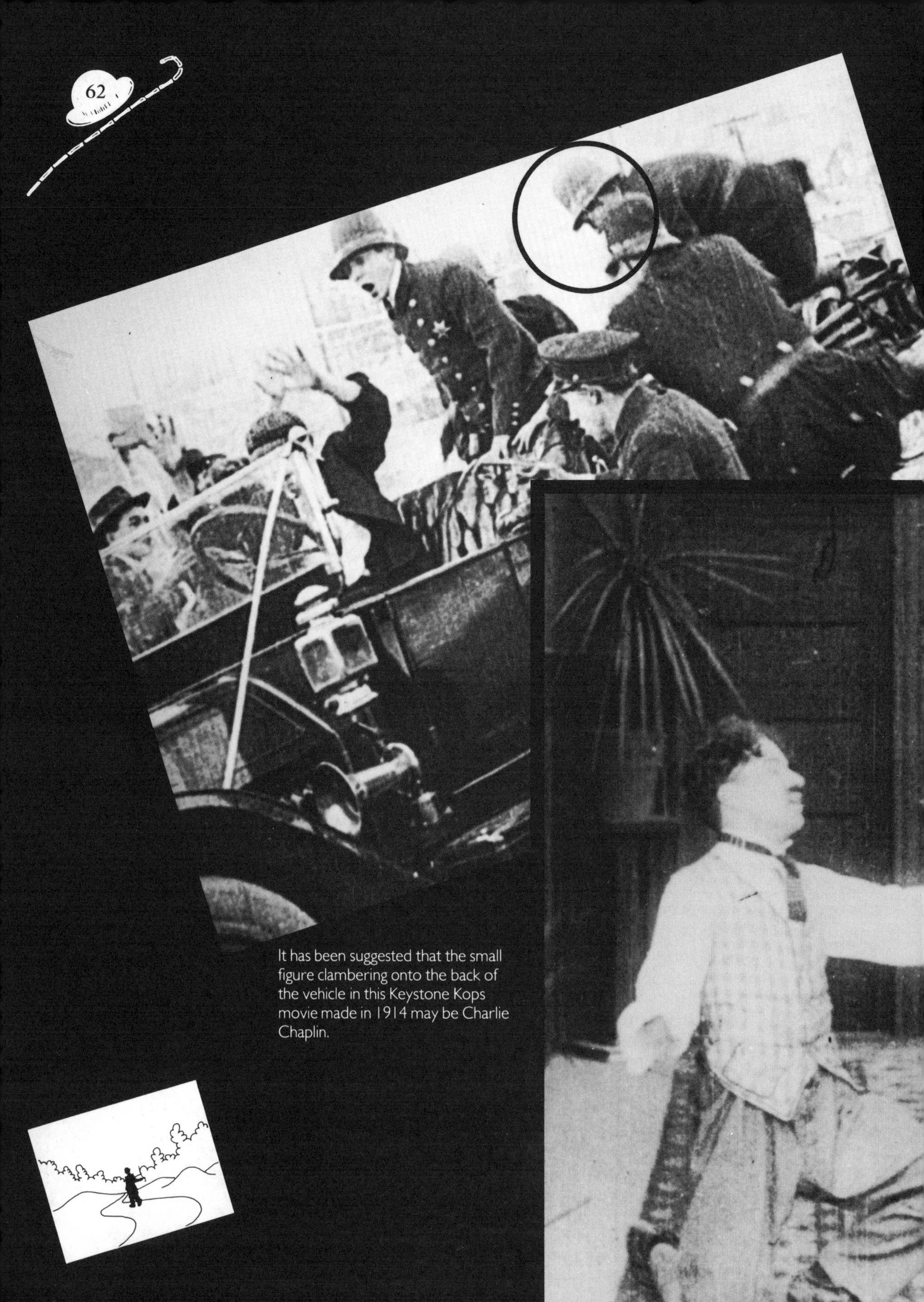

It has been suggested that the small figure clambering onto the back of the vehicle in this Keystone Kops movie made in 1914 may be Charlie Chaplin.

Charlie in *Mabel's Strange Predicament* (1914) which Henry Lehrman directed for Keystone. Mabel Normand is the girl and Harry McCoy the rival suitor.

A far cry from the Little Tramp! Charlie in *Tango Tangles* which he made under Mack Sennett's supervision in 1914. His co-stars were Ford Sterling, Fatty Arbuckle and Minta Durfee.

HOW CHARLIE WON THROUGH

Charlie's first publicist in America was a former English journalist turned actor named Fred Goodwins whom he had met when both men were employed by the impressario Charles Frohman. Goodwins was actually on a vaudeville tour of the States in 1915 when he was offered the chance of joining Charlie's little band of stock artists at the Essanay studios. He subsequently appeared in a number of films including *A Night Out*, *A Jitney Elopement*, *The Tramp*, *The Bank*, and most notably in *Police*, in the dual role of a preacher and a policeman. With the growing demand for information about Chaplin as his fame spread, it was second nature for Goodwins to take up his pen, and among the articles he wrote was the 'ghosted' essay under Chaplin's by-line, 'Fooling For The Film' which was syndicated to magazines in America and Britain in the autumn of 1915 and is reprinted in this book. The re-publication here marks its first return to print, and though fanciful to a degree, is nonetheless interesting because of Goodwins' involvement in the making of the Chaplin movies. In 1920, during a visit to London, Fred Goodwins gave a lecture at the Stoll Theatre about Charlie's conquest of Hollywood and also settled the little matter of who it was first spotted Charlie's screen potential and how the Little Tramp's outfit was devised . . .

'It was five and a half years ago while Charlie was on tour in America with 'Mumming Birds' that he received a letter from two men called Adam Kessel and Charles Bauman, names that were unknown to him. Kessel had apparently seen his act and been impressed.

'Charlie got in touch with the two men and discovered that they represented the Keystone Film Company. After an exchange of letters, he signed up for £40 a week and went to California.

'But his first attempts at filming, *Making A Living* and *Kid Auto Races at Venice*, were failures. He was in great earnest, and pointed out that whereas his humour was of the English type, he was in the hands of a Continental director (Henry Lehrman), and, after some parley, a compromise was effected, by which he was to undertake the direction of his own pictures.

'He chose his own wardrobe for the experiment, and fell on the old felt hat and a tight little morning coat. He borrowed Fatty Arbuckle's trousers and shoes, taking off the heels, and then, with

One of the postcards issued by Essanay to publicise their new star, Charlie Chaplin.

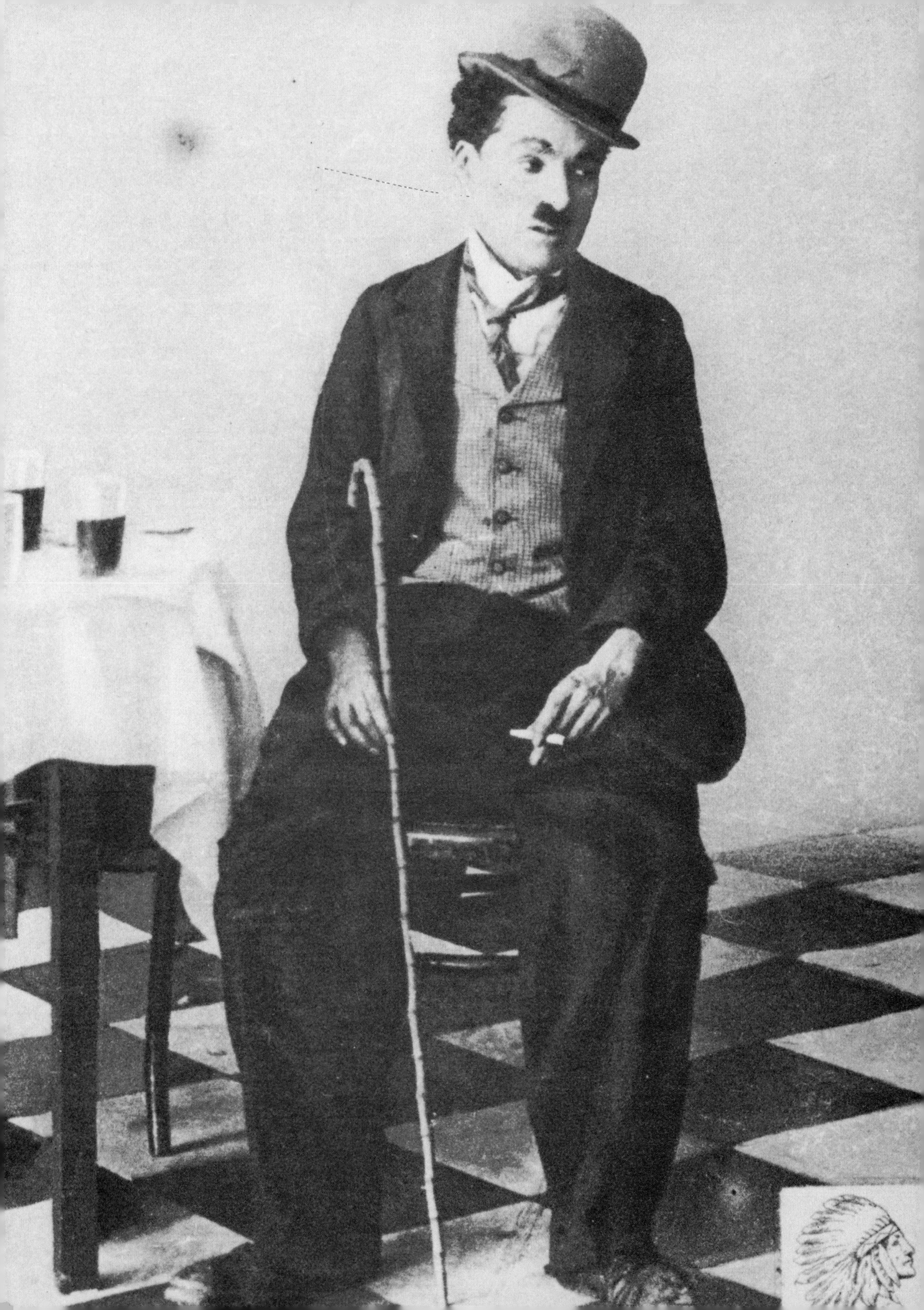

Fred Goodwins with Charlie in *The Tramp*, made for Essanay in 1915.

a wangee cane and moustache, he was complete. He was famous by the end of the year and when his contract expired had many offers.

'But Chaplin was always a sporting spirit. He gave his first refusal to the Keystone people, and when they would not accept, Essanay (George Spoor and 'Broncho Billy' Anderson) got him for £230 a week. At Niles, San Francisco, he worked for seven months and made *Charlie's Night Out*, *Champagne Charlie*, *Charlie the Tramp* and *Charlie's Elopement*.

'Charlie's ambition was to do a comedy drama feature, and in May 1915, he started a six-reeler, *Life*. It was at this time that I met him again and left my job in the legitimate theatre with a

Frohman company to join him making pictures. There was such a demand for two-reel comedies that *Life* had to be shelved.

'In February 1916 when *Police* was finished, Chaplin went to New York, where he was fêted for six weeks, and then signed a record contract for £2,000 a week and a cash bonus of £30,000 with the Mutual Film Company to do twelve pictures in twelve months.

'He took 18 months to do them, in fact, but gave the surplus six months' services free because he never sacrificed his art for money, and would spare no pains to get good results.

'Charlie Chaplin is, in my opinion, one of the true artists of the screen, and the outstanding figure in the motion picture industry.'

Perhaps Fred Goodwins' most notable appearance in an Essanay picture as a preacher in *Police* (1916). The drunk is played by James T. Kelley.

FOOLING FOR THE FILM

This essay, which carried Charlie's by-line, was written by Fred Goodwins, and one wonders whether Chaplin agreed to the artistic licence it contains. For herein the reader will learn the remarkable 'facts' that Chaplin considered himself a serious actor, disliked his 'get-up' of baggy trousers, bowler hat and cane, and actually got his inspiration for the Little Tramp from a real-life American hobo he had a fight with! It is a typical example, in fact, of how the facts and fictions of Charlie's life became entangled over the years.

At last I arrived at the studio of the film company that, so I told myself, had been foolish enough to want me as one of their comedians. They little knew the serious type of actor they were getting, as I told the manager who was giving me good advice.

'What we want, my boy,' he said, 'is down-right humour and sheer good fun – something that will make the people scream and laugh.'

Then, as he looked at my face, he roared with laughter.

'I don't know quite what it is,' he said, 'but that expression of gloom on your countenance is about the funniest thing I have ever seen outside a mortuary.'

I shuffled uneasily. I was going to be an entire failure; I could see that.

'Now, then,' said the manager, 'you take this little scenario, and have a good look over it. You see what you have to got to do. It's all written down there.'

THE LADDER WAS GREASED

I took the manuscript and departed, a prey to gloomy forebodings. The manager had spoken about breaking up houses and destroying cisterns. He had told me that he got a lot of humour out of that kind of thing. Murder struck him as being the funniest thing in the world, I fancy.

Let me just tell you what I did in my first film.

I had to play the part of a man with a limp and a backache, who was trying to carry a scuttle of coals on his head while he was climbing a greasy ladder.

I had been arrayed in a pair of baggy trousers, a little bowler and

a tiny cane – a get-up that I distinctly disliked. I put the coal-scuttle on my head, and nimble always on my feet, I commenced my climb.

I would not let them see me slip on the first few rungs, I told myself. I meant, if possible, to get through the whole business without falling. Up and up I went, my face pouring with perspiration, with behind me that insistent camera whir.

MADE A DISTINCT 'HIT'

It was just as I got to the top that something went wrong with the works. The coal-bucket upturned, and chunks of heavy material came banging all over my head. Then my hands slipped, and I just slid down the long ladder and glared indignantly at the producer.

He roared with laughter till he couldn't speak. I expect it was my gloomy face and woebegone-looking figure.

I was wrath, I can tell you, but I meant to get a bit of my own back. Suddenly I picked up a lump of coal, and slung it at the producer. It hit him full and fair on the nose, and the camera man actually included it in the film. Next I lifted one of my feet, and caught a stage hand who was gurgling near by a biff in what I have now learned to call the bazooka. He fell back into a pail of whitewash, while his friends ran for safety.

I was chucking coal right and left now. To use an East Endism, 'my monkey was up.' I would teach them to laugh at me!

THE MANAGER APPROVED

My first attempt at cinema acting was a noisy one. I brought the house down – at least, the greater part of it, for the great electric globes I broke with coal. I put a couple of stage hands' eyes out

Charlie in a spot of bother with two holidaymakers he has upset in *By The Sea,* made for Essanay in 1915. The co-stars are Billy Armstrong and Bud Jamison.

A hilarious moment from Charlie's film, *Work* (1915) in which he played a decorator's apprentice. His sorely-tried boss is Charles Insley.

of action, and paralysed the producer; while the camera operator had to go to hospital for a week for laughing too hard.

The result was that I was called up before the boss the next day, and told that if I went on like that I was made for life!

'There's a fortune in the way you chuck coal,' he said; 'but we'll make it bricks in future, Charlie. You can throw to your heart's content, but for Heaven's sake not when I'm about. Oh, then, there's another thing,' he added. 'I want you to roam round finding types. Choose someone that strikes your fancy, and then work a little play round him. Follow his characteristics, and so on.'

It was the 'so on' that led me to a pretty little fight in a nearby park a couple of days later. I noticed a tramp-like individual who was lounging on a seat, and busily devouring some hunks of bread. He was wearing huge boots that struck me as being pictures in their way – moving pictures.

HE WAS 'SOME' SCRAPPER

I sat down and watched him, and when he proceeded on his journey, followed at a discreet distance. We came to a bend in one of the paths, and, passing round this, I could see him come up to a dainty girl who was watching some swans in the lake.

Very cheekily he raised his hat, and tried to get into conversation with her. She looked rather pale, so I hurried forward just as the tramp caught at her hand.

'Take your hands off,' I said abruptly. But I was not prepared for the Nemesis that suddenly caught me in the centre of gravity, and shot me a few yards away.

The tramp's feet had let out like piston-rods, and he gently raised his hat to me. I was not thinking so much then of the value that this particular type would be as for vengeance when I gave chase.

A spirited little fight ensued – a fight in which I must frankly admit, the tramp had the advantage. To use an Americanism, he was 'some' scrapper. He used every part of his body, from his feet, which were like a couple of riverside barges, to his bullet-like head, with which he butted me at moments when the fight was going against him. He hit me everywhere, and I was not sorry when at last he sheered off.

THE MAN WITH THE PISTOL

I can see him now as he politely raised his bowler and vanished in the distance. It was from that character that I evolved the Charlie Chaplin that you know. During that fight I had carefully watched the evolution of my enemy's feet. The boss wanted blue murder of the knockabout kind; if there was anything qualified to give it, it would be those feet of my friend, the enemy.

I put him into the next little play that I did, and it was an enormous success immediately. But some of the actors with whom I played strongly objected to the use of those feet that caught them in such unexpected places.

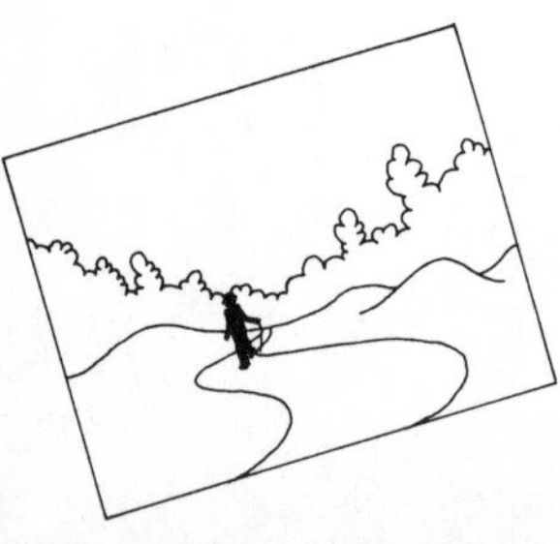

'Charlie,' said the boss, when we had filmed the thing to a finish, 'you're a wonder. Get some more types!'

Oh, those were happy days! Full of action, I can tell you, especially on one occasion when following one old gentleman of ninety, who had a peculiar gait that pleased my eye, he turned and let go at me with a six-shooter, and then tried to kiss me. He had escaped from a nearby asylum, and I nearly went to one that night. But I finally recovered from the fright I had, and – well, I put him into a play!

ALL IN THE DAY'S WORK

Life was one constant round of excitement, but I discovered that this knockabout work, although it brought success, was not the most pleasant form of occupation. To you it may seem amusing when someone taps me on the head with a mallet or lifts me a few hundred yards with an upper-cut. But it doesn't appeal to me as funny.

I remember a kick I got from a horse that sent the company into fits of laughter, and me to a sick ward for a couple of days; but there, that is all part of the game. We are all players, and we have to play our parts whether they are dangerous or not.

One of the funniest things that has followed my success on the films has been the flood of proposals that I have had from various of the fair sex. There was one old lady who remembered me in her

A montage of moments from *The Champion* drawn by Frank R. Grey in 1915.

will, and left me a canary and the family Bible. But there was one girl who invited me to meet her at a teahouse. She was very fascinating, and I went.

It was during the meal that a very tall, dark individual, with a couple of fists like a bulldog's snout, came to the next table, and looked daggers at me. I commented upon this new arrival to the girl. She only laughed.

'D'you know him?' I said, anxiously eyeing the stalwart starer.

'Oh, yes,' she replied, stuffing her handkerchief into her mouth to stifle her mirth. 'He's only my husband!'

WHEN SEEN ON THE SCREEN

When she had turned I had vanished like a streak of lightning into the distance, and I have made inquiries since before keeping appointments with unknown girls.

These things all add to the excitement of a film actor's life. It is a curious existence, being funny to a silent audience – sometimes that is, for occasionally even the people who are filming the play can hardly restrain their laughter. And I notice an extraordinary thing, that, although during parts of my performance I may be struck with the funny side of my work, whenever I see one of my films shown on the screen I find laughter very difficult.

I was very glum once in a picture palace watching a film at which everybody was laughing, much to the anger of an old gentleman sitting next to me. But that is another story, and no doubt now he tells of the silent individual who lacks a sense of humour, little knowing that it was Charlie Chaplin.

But I thank goodness for the fact that sometimes I can be funny, as once taken by a detective friend of mine, I found myself witnessing an evening of entertainment at a dancing-hall in the Bowery district of New York.

SAVED BY THE TANGO

They don't like strangers in these places, and somehow they picked myself and my friend out as being interlopers. It looked as though there was going to be some shooting, for a dark-looking Dago with an ominous knife in his belt was squaring up to me, when, exerting all my efforts, I tried to imagine myself in a film play.

I ran round the room with the gait you know so well, and ended by climbing the hangings of the curtain, and finished the evening off by dancing the tango in the most burlesque manner possible to imagine.

I verily believe I saved my skin, for soon we had that place roaring with laughter, and when my friend and I left, it was to the cheers of the biggest band of cut-throats I have ever had the ill-fortune to look upon!

MAX LINDER - 'THE MASTER'

Charlie with Max Linder, the French pioneer film comic he called 'The Master'.

Max Linder battling an inanimate object – a bouquet of flowers – in just the style that Chaplin was to adopt. The film is *Max: Champione de Boxe*, which he made in 1910.

When Charlie began his film career in Hollywood, another emigrant from the other side of the Atlantic was already established as an internationally famous screen comedian, though few remember him today. He was the Frenchman, Max Linder, who was destined to remain the best known film comic until the outbreak of the First World War. Born in 1883 and initially a dramatic actor with the Theatre des Variétés, he began to make movies in 1905 for Pathé Films, developing the *persona* of a gallant and indestructible dandy who finds himself in one disorderly situation after another. One of Chaplin's most respected biographers, David Robinson, paid this tribute to Linder on the Centenary of his birth in December 1983:

'Linder was established as a star even before Chaplin joined the Fred Karno musical hall comedy troupes; and his career was already on the wane by 1914 when Chaplin made his first films. In that time, however, Linder had built up a treasury of visual comedy which has continued to serve his successors – Chaplin included – down to the present day. It is hard to discover a comedy plot or a single gag that is not anticipated in the 500 or more short comedies of his prolific output.'

René Jeanne, the equally distinguished French cinema historian, has underlined this statement: 'Charlie Chaplin owes Linder at least three ideas for scenarios, not to mention a particular manner of conducting an action, of keeping a *leit-motiv* running through a scene, of making the incredible appear believable and of giving verisimilitude to an indescribable idea.' It is also true to say that as Chaplin emerged to eclipse all other comedians, it was Max Linder's fate to have his career halted by the onset of World War One. Badly injured in the conflict and unable to recapture past glories, the Frenchman committed suicide with his wife in 1925. A naturally modest man, Linder gave the following impressions of Chaplin at work shortly after returning to Paris from a further visit to Hollywood in 1922:

'Charlie Chaplin calls me his teacher, but, for my part, I have been lucky to get lessons at his school. Charlie, like the true humourist he is, has studied laughter with care, and knows how to provoke it with the rarest precision. He leaves nothing to the chance of improvisation. He goes over and over scenes until he is satisfied. He shoots every single rehearsal and has them thrown on the screen several times so he may find the flaw which spoils the effect he is striving after. He keeps on starting again until he is content, and he is harder to please than his most harshly critical spectator.

'Seeing Charlie at work, I realise more clearly than ever how little count should be taken of the amount of negative that is used in making a picture. In France, we count the number of feet as if it had some connection with the finished article. But in reality the only thing that has any connection with the quality of the film is the care taken in producing the picture. To give exact figures on this point, Chaplin spent two months in making a picture of 1,800 feet and he used for that 35,000 feet of film negative!

'As a producer, he is deliberate and richly gifted. Spectators of every race and every type of mind can follow the evolution of his thought and the very finest touches of his wit. His imitators succeed in executing the same tricks as he does, but why do they not provoke the same laughter? Imitation is merely a proof of inferiority and impotence. Chaplin has a special get-up. He is famous by his own physique and gait. He is a genre of his own. Take all that from him if you will – it is only a pointless theft.'

Charlie looking the spitting image of Max Linder as a city slicker in his very first movie, *Making A Living,* which he filmed in January 1914.

Interestingly, for the past 30 years, Maud Linder, the star's only child, has been busy resurrecting those of Max's films that still exist, as well as publicising his achievements and importance in the history of screen comedy. She gave the following fascinating interview in Paris on the eve of her father's centenary.

'My father, Max Linder, was the first international comic film star and undoubtedly exerted a considerable influence on the development of American silent comedy – Mack Sennett and Charlie Chaplin in particular. He was also the first to introduce a natural style of acting in the cinema – the comedy of character – in contrast to the theatrical mannerisms of the time.

'Max Linder turned to comedy in 1905 on realising his small stature was not cut out for drama. In his first starring role, *Débuts D'un Patineur*, he played an elegantly dressed gentleman who tries to skate on a frozen lake. Because he can't skate, he keeps tumbling over and the resulting scenes started his rise to fame.

'Thereafter he perfected his character into that of an elegant gentleman complete with black frock coat, striped trousers, spats and patent shoes, yellow gloves, silk hat, a moustache and a swagger cane. His hundreds of short pictures were made all over Europe, including France, Spain and even Russia. Some were filmed in a day, others a week! The French people loved them.

'It was in 1916 that the Essanay Company invited Max to America to make some films for them, and there he met and befriended Charlie Chaplin who had already seen some of his pictures while he was travelling with the Karno troupe in both France and America.

'Chaplin acknowledged his debt to my father by inscribing on a photograph: "To the one and only Max, The Professor. From his Disciple, Charlie Chaplin. May 12, 1917." On another occasion he made a reference to, "Max Linder, who taught me my job." Yet, if you read Chaplin's autobiography, he makes no mention of his "teacher" at all!

'I know there are many historians who are sceptical about claims that Max Linder influenced Chaplin. But, for example, look at the appearance of Chaplin in his first film, *Making A Living*, where his clothes are exactly the same dapper outfit as Linder had been wearing for half a dozen years. And there is a short film, dating from the year 1907, in which Max, cane in hand, executes a walk that is identical to the one Chaplin introduced in 1914.

'The Marx Brothers also owe Max a debt. That famous scene with the broken mirror in *Duck Soup* (1933) was actually devised by my father for his picture, *Seven Years' Bad Luck*, made in 1921!

'In his day, Max Linder was described as "the funniest man in the world" – a title which Chaplin inherited when tragedy over-

The portrait photograph which Charlie inscribed so warmly to Max Linder as the 'one and only'.

whelmed my father. He volunteered his services to his country at the outbreak of the First World War and fell victim to a poison gas attack while he was in the trenches. His health was never the same, and I am convinced that unbalanced his mind.

'Fortunately, I have been able to recover some 80 of his films and the comedy in them is still fresh and funny, and they could find a new audience through re-release. After all, Chaplin has his admirers, and I believe the man he once called "My Master" richly deserves his, too!'

REUNITED BY A RED RAVEN SPLIT

Chester Courtney was an English vaudeville comic and contemporary of Charlie Chaplin who knew him well in London and was then re-united with the star by chance in Hollywood – a meeting which lead to Courtney appearing in several of the pictures the Little Tramp made for Mutual Films in 1916–7 including *The Floorwalker*, *The Count* and *The Pawnbroker*. In February 1931, after he had returned to London, Courtney reminisced about his experiences with Chaplin on both sides of the Atlantic.

'I was a singer with Park's Eton Boys and Chaplin was a knockabout with Karno's Mumming Birds when we first met. That was in 1910: he was 21 and I was 17. We appeared at the same halls on half a dozen different occasions and became intimately acquainted. He was a boy with vague ideas about life, but no concrete visions of either his future or his desires. Films, as a career, never occurred to him.

'That he would drift out of the rough-and-tumble, happy-golucky environment in which I first found him was only sketchily probable, for in those days vaudeville was a professional tree with many ripe prizes waiting to be picked, and I believe he had ideas about succeeding as a star comedian. That he had a mind was evident, but it was uncultivated soil sown with nothing but the weeds of a back-alley childhood, a childhood devoid of books, romance or anything but the rawest edges of London life. He was half-educated and underfed, his views of life narrowed by the archways of Kennington through which he had always peeped.

'Yet there were moments when he gave voice to whimsical thoughts and visionary notions – beautiful imaginings that gave one the impression some delicate flower had blossomed overnight in the grey, weed-covered patch that was his uncultivated mind.

'We shared common amusements – twopenny poker, promiscuous flirtations, Woodbines and bus rides. Woodbines were his favourite cigarettes. Years later, when his income had extended beyond his reckoning, when a dozen brands of expensive cigarettes were advertising his "unsolicited testimonials", he continued to fish familiar little green packets from odd corners of his clothes. He had them sent to him in thousands all through the War, and is reported to have smoked Woodbines at a New York banquet!

'There are other quaint pictures of him that run through my

Chester Courtney, the former English vaudeville performer who was dramatically reunited with Charlie in America.

mind, pictures as whimsical as those of his screen fame, yet they are glimpses of his real self, the man behind the clown. I knew both Charlie and Charles and there is a considerable difference.

'Charlie became Charles when the raw-boned, half-baked globe-trotting vaudevillian turned into a rich international notability, polished and refined by his continual shoulder-rubbing with the cultured and the genteel.

'One memory picture of Charlie shows him pressing a pair of trousers, soiled, shiny trousers, in order that he might join me in an evening ramble along Brixton Road in search of feminine adventures. Arm-in-arm we used to stroll from the Bon Marché to the foot of Brixton Hill, winking and chi-iking and signalling, until we encountered a pair of roving damsels who satisfied our taste in intellect and beauty. (Beauty first and foremost in those days!) A flirtatious chat on the pavement edge, a stroll up Brixton Hill, or a bus ride followed.

'Another mental image depicts Charlie sitting on an old iron bed in Kennington, his feet dangling, his hair unruly, his white fingers carefully separating a Woodbine in order that I might not go smokeless. Isn't that a glimpse that might have been snipped from one of his films?

'In a third mind-picture I see him as a shabbily dressed kid in a knockabout gang, vainly trying to honestly eke out a frail income by the manipulation of dirty cards in a twopenny poker game.

'In fact, my last recollection of him in his 'Mumming Bird' days was a picture of his slim figure on a rickety old hamper in a suburban dressing-room, his bright eyes fastened intently on a few greasy cards, his white fingers selecting, shuffling and flipping; his pale, sensitive face topped by that cluster of tousled hair.

'The next time I saw him he was seated on a bed at the Los Angeles Athletic Club while two detectives guarded his bedroom door. I, in the uniform of a bell-boy, had just entered with a Red Raven Split. The unbelieving expression on his face as he recognised me was quainter than any I ever saw in his films!

'Six years had passed, during which time he had visited America with 'Mumming Birds', had been seen and booked by Mack Sennett, made his Keystone successes, concluded the Essanay contract, and just signed a starring agreement with Mutual Films at the largest salary ever paid to an individual in American films! I, for what it concerns this story, had sung in the London streets, worked a passage to New York, sold papers on Broadway, and bought myself, for $20, a job as the Bell Hop at the Los Angeles Athletic Club. His order for a Red Raven Split had brought us face to face again. He was sucking an orange when I entered.

'"Charlie!" I yelled. He looked up, expressed half a dozen emotions in one, dropped the orange and seized my hand. For two hours we sat side by side on the bed and talked. He asked me a thousand questions about London, particularly about Kennington. And all the while, down below, the Bell-Hop Captain was going frantic. Three times he came to the door, but Charlie's detectives would not let him in. Mr Chaplin was "in conference".

'Every few moments, as we dug up some drab and tattered picture from the past, he would exclaim, "Happy days . . . happy

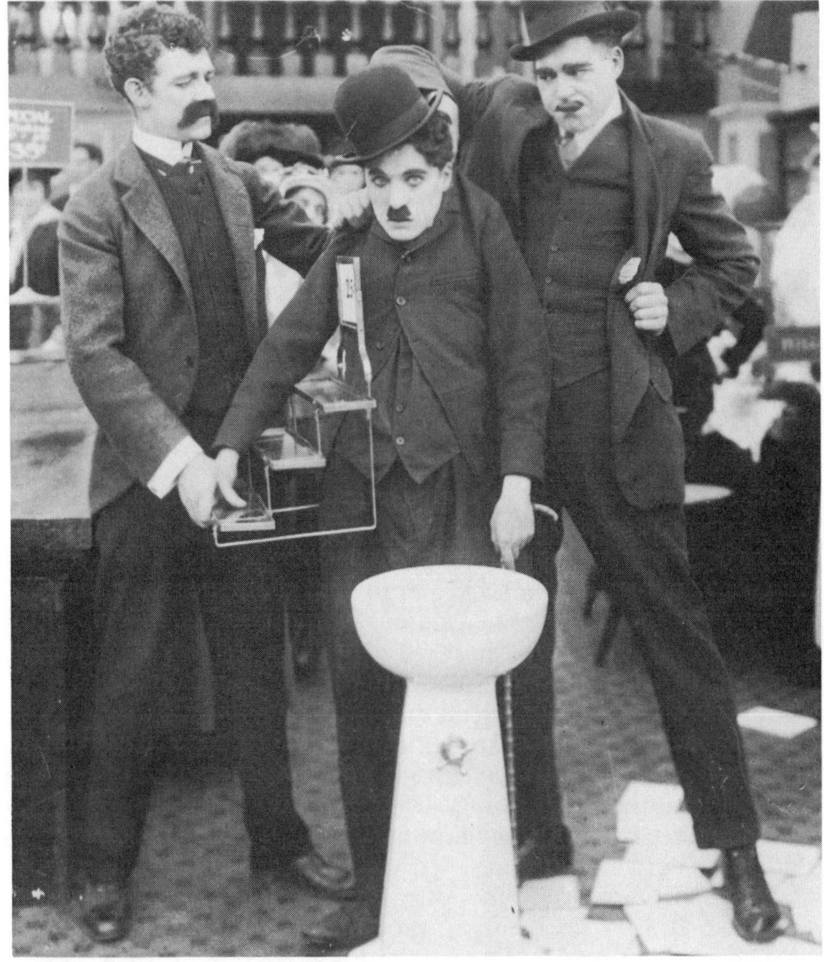

The Floorwalker, Charlie's first picture for Mutual Films, in which Chester Courtney also appeared. Albert Austin is the shop assistant (left) and Tom Nelson the detective.

days!" He was a rich man, with every kind of luxury within his reach, while the periods he resurrected were unrelieved stretches of grey poverty.

'He made me take off my uniform and sent for my private clothes. Half an hour later we were crossing the lobby, arm-in-arm; while 14 bell boys, an elevator man, the office staff and the Bell Captain gaped.

'As we reached the swing doors, the Captain growled, "You're fired." A moment later we reached the sidewalk. "You're engaged," said Charlie, and marched me right into the studios!

'Although he had signed with the Mutual Company, he had not yet commenced his first film. When I started work at the studio next morning, to my surprise I found the staff idle. Charlie was in conference with himself, I was informed. He was indulging in *Thought*. And since everything in a Chaplin film emanates from the brain of Chaplin, nothing but his mind moves when he is in the throes of mental resolution.

'A week passed. The studio was silent, the staff idle, the executives worried and nervous. Charles, a thin, wistful figure, paced the streets and the studio floor. "Not big enough," he would say, when we ventured suggestions. Then the big idea struck him accidentally.

A scene from *Easy Street* (1917), the set for which Charlie based on the road in London where he was born.

'He was standing in Hamburger's department store, Los Angeles. The escalator was running. His eyes seized on it and remained riveted. His mind began to revolve. In it he saw himself at the head of a chase on the running stairway; he and his pursuers going down while the elevator rolled up.

'He ran to the phone. "Build me a moving stairway," he commanded, while at the other end the studio manager scribbled hasty notes. "And set up a department store around it!" From that was born *The Floorwalker*, one of his greatest successes.

'There was never anything definite or precise about Charlie's hours or his work. He would lounge all day, keeping his staff and studio idle, and then wake the whole outfit at 1 a.m. and command them to start work! Once he roused all the carpenters at midnight and ordered a set for breakfast time. It was ready. Sometimes he worked at white heat and kept us at it day and night for weeks.

'He would order sets costing five, seven and ten thousand dollars, and then ignore them, working in odd corners or against converted backgrounds rigged up at an hour's notice. One night he struck an idea and ordered a $10,000 dollar set to be built at once. It was finished in record time. He used it three pictures later! It formed the basis of *Easy Street*.

'Writing scenarios for Chaplin was a waste of time. He always improvised and changed the plot a dozen times. He would start with one outline, branch into another, strike a third idea and scrap the other two. It was impossible to keep pace with him. He thought faster than all the express brains in Hollywood. If you told him an idea he saw the end before you had finished outlining the beginning, and was improving the whole before you were halfway through!

'During the period of my association, he hit on the notion that he would not only discard his comical accessories, but also his human supporters. The vision of a solo picture took complete possession of him and we spent a delightful week playing craps and poker while he mooned around the studio, thinking. The picture *One A.M.* grew out of that.

I sat beside him in the Garrick Theatre, Los Angeles on the night of its initial showing. All round us the frenzied audience

Charlie and Edna Purviance, the former stenographer he made a star – and with whom Chester Courtney was convinced he was in love. They are seen here in a tender moment from *Shoulder Arms* (1918).

showered compliments. Charlie, unhearing, sat in moody contemplation of the screen.

'"What do you think of it?" he asked, to which I replied, "Wonderful. What's your own opinion?"

'"One more film like that," he answered, "and it will be Goodbye Charles!"

'Only those who have worked beside Charlie know how clever he can be. I have told you that he schemes his own plots, designs his own sets, creates his own comedy. But there is more.

'Unexpectedly, in the middle of a day's shooting, he suddenly produced chalks and paper and began to draw. No one had ever seen him draw before. He sketched men, women and animals. He caricatured his staff, his friends and himself. He drew for our benefit until night fell.

'He is also a musician and a composer. I still have a published song bearing on the cover these words, "Oh, That 'Cello!" by Charles Chaplin.

'The mention of music reminds me of another occasion when I almost lost my sanity thanks to Charlie – indeed, if anyone plays 'They Call it Dixieland' in my hearing I run off screaming. You see, he kept a studio band playing it for three weeks, almost without a break. He was learning to dance, with Edna Purviance, and the result of his patience (and ours, for I wonder we didn't brain him) was shown to the world in *The Count*.

'During the filming of *The Pawnbroker* he held up the schedule for two weeks while he learned to play all the instruments that the property man, Scotty Cleethorpes, had provided for the shop scene, in which they figured as pledged goods. When the end of the fortnight came he gave us an impromptu concert at which he played one tune on each instrument!

'There is a boy's game called 'Egg in the Hat' which involves caps, balls and stones. I doubt if you will ever see it played anywhere outside a school yard – or a Chaplin studio. The little clown held up *The Pawnbroker* while we all played 'Egg in the Hat'. But more than one Chaplin success was born in his brain while he aped kids!

'His interest in children, in fact, amounts almost to a passion. He understands the child mind better than any psychologist. To this comprehension you may set down much of his success with the juveniles in his audience. I have known him watch children at play hour after hour. From their natural actions and antics he derived many of his own whimsicalities. Jackie Coogan may thank Charles Chaplin's love of the kiddies for his own fame and fortune.

'On the other hand, I do not think any Hollywood star has had so many women in love with him as Charlie! It is extremely difficult to say whether he loved any of the many women who met, kissed or passed him. He may have given his heart to Pola Negri, Merna Kennedy, Georgia Hale or all of them. I do not know. I do not think anyone knows, the women least of all. Perhaps Charlie is as ignorant as the rest of us.

'But of all the women who worshipped at his feet during the time I knew him, I believe there was only one who understood him, the Californian ex-stenographer named Edna Purviance. And I believe he loved her.

'I form my judgement on the hundred and one little side lights that were revealed to me during my months in the Mutual Studios, when she was his star and constant companion; his adviser, his friend and his comforter. She understood him to the n'th degree. She humoured, anticipated and adored him. When he was moody (and when he was not) she treated him with patient tolerance. When he felt the urge to work she inspired and encouraged him; when he wanted to play she threw on a mantle of juvenile absurdity and joined in the pranks.

Charlie, of course, turned the awkward stenographer into a polished leading lady, but only those who, like myself, were present during the process know how hard he slaved to do it. He literally perspired over his attempts to mould her into an actress. More than once he lost his temper. A lesser man would have given up. But Charlie is a man of purpose, and his objective was to turn an office girl into a film actress. He succeeded. I consider her the most effective leading lady of his many.

'And I venture the bold statement that Charlie made the mistake of his private life when he passed Edna Purviance over in his selection of a wife. She would have been a loyal and invaluable helpmate, a splendid mother, an intelligent companion, a devoted pal. All Mutual knew that he had made an error, all Mutual sympathised with him in his loss.

'Edna was, I recall, involved in what I can only call one of his moments of genius. His histrionic gifts as seen on the screen require no description; but he actually has no need of the illusion created by cameras, lights and accessories to reach you with his talents of comedy or pathos. I have seen a studio crew weeping – the reaction to a simple piece of rehearsal acting.

'In *The Vagabond*, when he parted from the rich man's daughter, he had an effective and touching scene. I witnessed this being shot. Both Charlie and Edna were in tears, and, as he took his last farewell, lifted his narrow, pathetic shoulders in a wistful gesture of resignation and sloped away towards the evening light, there was not a tearless eye among the people who watched spellbound.'

Charlie reprising his role as a drunk in *One A.M*, which he made for Mutual in 1916.

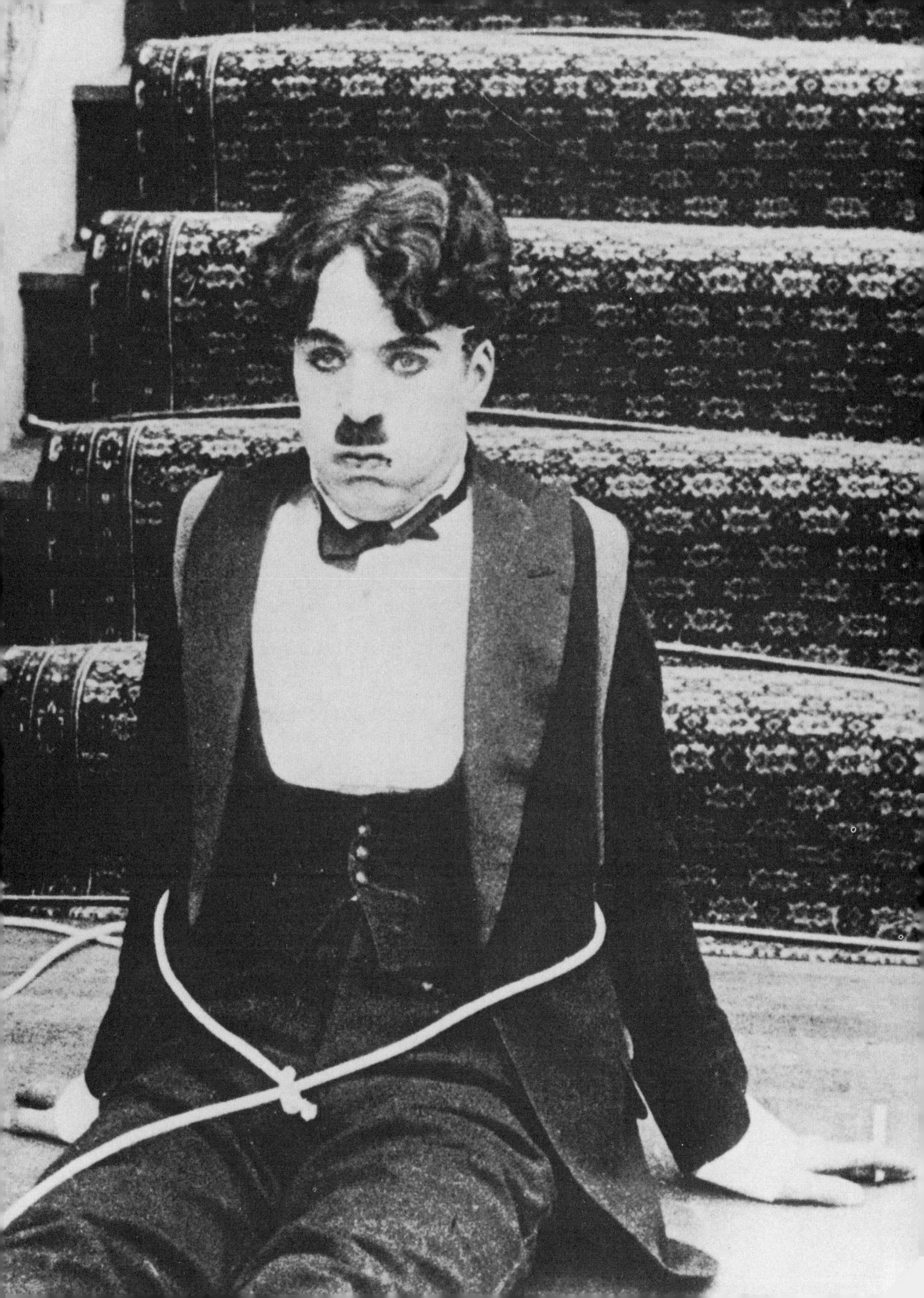

WHAT PEOPLE LAUGH AT

In the autumn of 1917, Charlie completed his contract with Mutual Films by making *The Adventurer*, and decided thereafter to work as an independent. To this end he built his own studios at 1416, North La Brea Avenue, just off Sunset Boulevard, designing them to resemble a row of picturesque half-timbered English cottages. Here he was to produce, write and direct perhaps the greatest and most famous of his movies including *A Dog's Life* (1918), *Shoulder Arms* (1918), *The Kid* (1921), *The Gold Rush* (1925), *The Circus* (1928), *City Lights* (1931), *Modern Times* (1936) and *The Great Dictator* (1940). This landmark soon became a mecca for Charlie's admirers, and he daily ran the gauntlet of fans wanting to see him and try to discover the secret of his success. In an effort to satisfy this desire for information, Charlie wrote an article, 'What People Laugh At' which was published in the November 1918 issue of the prestigious magazine, *The American*. It is now returned to print here, providing a revealing insight into Chaplin's art by the master himself.

'What I rely on more than anything else is bringing the public before someone who is in a ridiculous and embarrassing position. Thus, the mere fact of a hat being blown away isn't funny in itself. What is, is to see its owner running after it, with his hair blown about and his coat tails flying. A man is walking along the street – that doesn't lend itself to laughter. But placed in a ridiculous and embarrassing position he becomes a cause of laughter to his fellow-creatures. Every comic situation is based on that.

A thoughtful Charlie on the set of *A Dog's Life*, the first picture he made for his own company in 1918.

'Comic films had immediate success because most of them showed policemen falling down drain-holes, stumbling into whitewash pails, falling out of carts and put to all kinds of botherations. Here are people who stand for the dignity of power, and often deeply imbued with this idea, being made ridiculous and getting laughed at, and the sight of *their* mishaps makes the public want to laugh twice as much as they would at only ordinary citizens undergoing the same transformations.

'And still funnier is the person in a ludicrous position who, in spite of it, refuses to admit that anything out of the ordinary is happening, and is obstinate in preserving his dignity. The best example is given by the drunken man who, though given away by his speech and his walk, wants to convince us that he has not

touched a drop. He is much funnier than the frankly merry gentleman who shows his drunkenness as plain as day.

'That is why all my films rest on the idea of getting myself into awkward situations, so as to give me the chance of being desperately serious in my attempts to look like a very normal little gentleman. That is why my chief concern, no matter how painful the position I get myself into, is always to pick up my little cane at once, and put my bowler hat straight, and adjust my necktie – even if I've just fallen on my head. I am so sure of this that I do not try only to get myself into these embarrassing positions, but I count on putting others also into them.

'When I work on this principle I make every effort to economise my means. I mean by this that when one single happening can by itself arouse two separate bursts of laughter, it's better than two separate happenings doing so. In *The Adventurer* I succeeded in placing myself on a balcony where I have to eat an ice with a young lady. On the floor beneath I place a stout, respectable, well-dressed lady, sitting at a table. Then, while eating my ice, I let fall a spoonful which slides down my trousers, and then falls from the balcony down the lady's neck. The first laugh is caused by my own embarrassment, the second, and much the greater, comes from the arrival of the ice on the lady's neck, and she screams and dances about. One single action has been enough, but it has made two people ridiculous and set laughter free twice.

'Simple as this seems, there are two traits of human nature

which it throws light on. One is the pleasure taken by the public in seeing richness and luxury in distress; the other is the tendency of the public to feel in itself the same emotions as the actor on the stage or the screen. One of the facts soonest learned in the theatre is that most people are rather pleased when they see rich folk having the worst time. This comes from the fact that nine out of ten human beings are poor and inwardly jealous of the riches of the tenth. Now if I had made my ice fall down the neck of some poor housewife, there would have been a burst of sympathy instead of laughter for the woman. Moreover, the incident wouldn't have been funny, because the housewife would have no dignity to lose. To let an ice fall down a rich woman's neck is, in the public's opinion, to let her have just what she deserves.

'The idea of the cane is perhaps my best find. For it is the cane that made me quickest known, and besides, I have elaborated its uses until it has acquired a comic character of its own. Often I find it hooked round someone's leg, or catching him by the shoulder, and so raising a laugh almost without my noticing the act myself. I don't think I quite knew at first how true it is that, for millions of individuals, a walking-stick marks a man as rather a "swell." And so when I come shuffling on to the scene with my little cane and my serious air, I give the impression of an attempt at dignity, and that is exactly my object.

'Obviously it is lucky for me that I am small and can get these contrasts without difficulty. Everyone knows that the persecuted

The famous balcony scene with Edna Purviance in *The Adventurer* (1917).

Charlie the awkward soldier in his classic First World War picture, *Shoulder Arms*.

little individual always has the sympathy of the crowd. Knowing this liking for the weakest, I contrive to emphasise my weakness by working my shoulders, and assuming a pitiable expression, and taking on a frightened air. All that, of course, is the art of pantomime; but if I were a little bigger I should have more trouble in winning sympathy, for I should then have been deemed capable of looking after myself. But as I am, the public, even while laughing at my appearance, really feels for me.

'Alongside contrast I put surprise. I do not strive for complete surprise in the general composition of a film, but I force myself to make my personal gestures come in some surprising form. I try always to create the unexpected in a new way. If I feel convinced that the public are expecting me to proceed along the street on foot, I jump into a cab. If I want to attract someone's attention, instead of touching his shoulder or calling him, I pass my cane round his arm and draw him gently towards me. To make the public think I'm going to do what they expect, and then to do just the opposite is a pure pleasure for me.

'One thing I have to guard against is exaggeration or putting too much reliance on a particular point. I could kill laughter more easily by exaggeration than in any other way. If I overdid my peculiar walk, if I were too brutal in knocking someone over, if I chanced on any excess, it would spoil the film.

'Self-restraint is of the utmost importance. . . . One reason why I dislike my early films is that restraint was difficult in them. One or two custard pies are amusing enough, perhaps, but when the picture depends on nothing else, it soon becomes a weariness.

'Perhaps I have not always succeeded by my methods, but I do prefer a thousand times to get a laugh by an intelligent act than by anything brutal or banal. There is no mystery in making the public laugh. My whole secret is in keeping my eyes open and my wits wide-awake for everything capable of being used in my films.'

'THE FILM SHAKESPEARE'

Apart from the fans who dogged Charlie's footsteps in Hollywood, many thousands more wrote to him from all the corners of the world where his films were now being shown. Chaplin himself was a notoriously bad correspondent, and probably wrote no more than a few dozen replies in his own hand during his lifetime. His business affairs and mail were handled by a specially appointed staff, among whose numbers was Elsie Codd, who gave years of devoted service coping with the avalanche of mail that arrived every day at the studios. One of Miss Codd's rewards was a small part in *The Kid* in 1921. A little earlier, on a return to her native England, she talked about Charlie's fan mail and some of the curious letters it contained.

'I suppose Charlie Chaplin's reputation as a funny man accounts for some of the funny things he gets in his mail.

'There is one lady, for instance, who writes to him regularly from the East. Apparently she is a believer in the theory of reincarnation, and is continually reminding Charlie by registered letter of some promise he made her in a previous existence to "bring the gods of the mastedons to light", though Charlie himself has no recollection of having in any way been associated with the writer during any of his previous sojourns on this earth!

'Another enthusiast thinks Charlie would make a sure fire hit as Hamlet, "if you were to take off your moustache and big feet!" He earnestly implores Charlie "to show the people that you are not as big a fool as they think you are, and that you can play something worth the money. *Then* they would appreciate your work."

'However, as a kind of balm to his wounded feelings, Charlie received by the very same mail a letter from Sweden addressed to "The Film Shakespeare Chaplin". Which shows that you can't please everybody!

'One applicant for a photograph wants "a picture of your real face" and offers the opinion that Charlie's career has been – "very easy. You got in just by your smile and your ways." Pessimistically, the writer concludes, "You are very lucky. I am unlucky."

'There is a wonderfully quaint charm in the tributes that reach Charlie from Japan.

'"How are you feeling nowaday?" one admirer writes. "I think you are healthy without fail. Whenever I see you on the film I feel

comfortable joke and my heart becomes very cheerfully. Would you like to send me your photograph? I am good boy".

'"Would you kindly send me your valuable photo?" pleads another. "I like to see your figure the style, and am very glorious to hung up your smiling face in my room."

'"I think there is nothing more comfortable to me than to see your face," declares a little girl from Chrysanthemum land, "even in my sleeping your charming style comforts me till the morning after, but I am a miserable one then when your style disappears."

'"I had unintentionally the clapping hand when your gallant figure was throwed on the screen," enthuses a High School student. "I write broken words. I am afraid you can read poor my letter. Perhaps you would be greatly pained if you received it. But excuse me, gentleman, I sympathise with you when I see your appearance."

'Here is an acknowledgement of a photograph: "I full with delight and the tenderest emotions. It is far more precious in my eyes than the costly jewels. I will conserve it forever."

'Naturally some of Charlie's correspondents are not entirely disinterested in their homage. A gentleman who evidently has Bolshevik ideas on the subject of the community of wealth, demands five thousand pounds by return for a little mining enterprise in which he is interested. Another announces that he has had the latest addition to his family christened Charles and as an afterthought throws in a postscript, "We are poor, but very proud."

One man wrote recently and wanted a suit! He was obviously a bit of a fad and would only consider a particularly expensive make. He stipulated, however, that the gift should remain anonymous, as his people did not like the idea of his "associating with moving picture actors." Can you beat it!

'If Charlie were to give away his wardrobe to all the persons who seem to stand in need of it, he would only have his screen regalia wherewith to appear on Broadway.

'One pathetic appeal he recently received revealed the fact that the writer was forced to keep to his bed for sheer lack of clothes, and yet paradoxically mentioned that he had seen *Sunnyside* five times that week! It is still a mystery to the Chaplin mind how that man managed to get past the keeper of the door.

'Possibly, however, the pearl of Charlie's fan mail is a letter which he is keeping against the time when he notices symptons of acquiring a swelled head.

'"I enjoy your work," the writer generously concedes, "but I should enjoy it more if you would be yourself and not always be trying to imitate Billy West!"'

(Billy West was a Jewish immigrant from Russia who became a vaudeville star and from 1915 made a speciality of imitating Chaplin. In 1916 he appeared in *His Waiting Career*, the first of a series of movies in which he impersonated the little tramp. In all West made over 50 short movies and was generally regarded as the best of the Chaplin imitators. By a stange quirk of fate, a supporting actor in a number of his early films was one Oliver Hardy, destined to become famous with Charlie's former colleague, Stan Laurel!)

CHARLES CHAPLIN TO DAY

OLD RUSH

BETTER BE YOURSELF, HOWEVER SIMPLE, THAN A COPY OF SOMEONE ELSE, HOWEVER GREAT.

IF YOU WANT TO LOOK LIKE CHARLIE CHAPLIN,

Let your hair grow long and curl it till it looks like this

Pull a bit of wool off the mat and stick under your nose,

Buy a pair of old boots, too big for you, and turn out your toes,

And then you'll look like Charlie Chaplin, only you won't be HIM.

By the Twenties, Charlie Chaplin had become a cult figure around the world – copied by other entertainers and fans alike. The Little Tramp became a favourite source of inspiration for cartoonists. This typical example appeared in *Pearsons Magazine* of September 1925. Postcards such as the example here (right) sold in their millions.

Another example of the Chaplin craze – talent contests to find the best imitators of the Little Tramp!

THE TRAGEDY BEHIND THE KID

The beautiful blonde actress, Mildred Harris, who at 17 became the first of Charlie's four wives.

In October 1918, while he was making his first anti-war picture, *Shoulder Arms*, Charlie married the first of his four wives, Mildred Harris, a 17-year-old blonde former child actress from Wyoming, of Welsh-English ancestry. Like Charlie, she was already a veteran stage performer by her early teens and made her screen debut at 15 in the D.W. Griffith picture, *Intolerance*. As a result of her marriage to Charlie, Mildred became internationally famous, but tragedy struck their union when their first child, a boy – and the heir Chaplin was so desperate to have – was born on July 7, 1919, but three days later Norman Spencer Chaplin was dead. The infant had been born severely handicapped, and when quietly buried in Ingelwood Cemetery on July 11 was laid under a gravestone with the simple inscription, 'The Little Mouse'. Though the couple divorced in 1920, to the day of her death, just a quarter of a century later on July 19, 1944, Mildred was convinced that the classic film Charlie began to work on immediately afterwards – and which many critics believe to be his greatest, *The Kid* – was directly inspired by this tragedy. In 1935, she recalled Charlie the husband and lover of children in an interview given in Hollywood.

'What is Charlie like as a husband? This droll, pathetically funny little man with the tramp clothes, whose pantomime had made him world famous – what sort of man is he to be wife to? Women in every country ask me this question – and I can tell them.

'He is jealous, intensely human, erratic, wonderfully sympathetic. He is not an individual – he represents a thousand phases of human existence: they have been gathered together, based on the vicissitudes that were his in early days, and presented to the world that hungers for alleviation.

'I forget all the heart-breaks and disappointments and disillusionments when I think of him as a father, a husband; a wistful look in his eyes born of solicitude for me and our child.

'That was the time when he forgot the fame and the adulation and revealed the tenderness of the man who understands.

'He adores children, and yearned for one of his own. I have seen him creeping almost stealthily into the confidence of street urchins at play. He has stood on his head for them and performed acrobatic tricks for their pleasure. Think of that – the great Charlie Chaplin, immensely wealthy, clowning in the gutter for

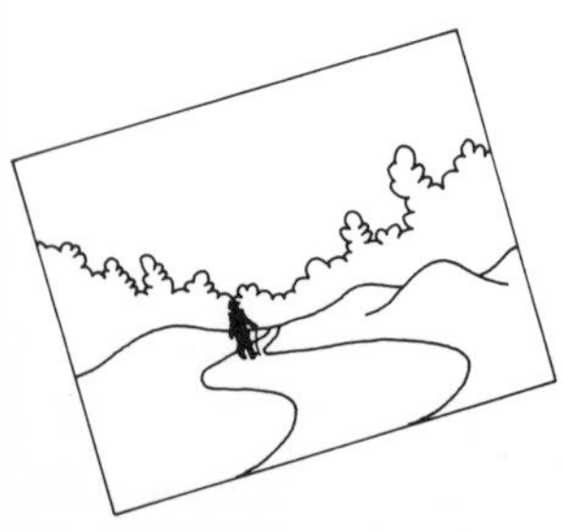

the entertainment of ragged children!

'Although Charlie was rich, money didn't mean very much to him, because he hadn't the time – his thoughts wouldn't allow it – to concentrate on the meaning of money.

'Our home life was as kaleidoscopic as a film play. His moods were ever changing; there were moments when triumph held him with its spell, and moments when doubts and fears pursued him relentlessly.

'Do you remember the story of the sad-faced little man who consulted a doctor saying that he was so depressed that he couldn't get a smile out of life? And the doctor saying, "Go to see Grimaldi, the greatest clown that ever lived."

'And the little man's answer, "I *am* Grimaldi!"

'I cannot help thinking of how easily that story might have been applied to Charles.

'First there was Californian sunshine and hopes. And then the cloud when our child died three days after he was born. I believe that if he had been spared I should still be the wife of Charles Chaplin today.

'I see again the look of anxiety on his face when the time came for me to be taken to the hospital for my confinement. The chauffeur was away and Charles himself rushed to the garage and got out the car.

'He wrapped me in a blanket, placed me in the car, and drove to the hospital. The doctors wished him to go away after I was safely installed there, but he insisted on staying and then – fainted! They carried him out.

'Charles was inconsolable over the death of his son. He had dreamed, yearned for a boy, and this seemed to add to the tragedy.

'I remember so clearly the day when I was ready to leave the hospital after the birth and death of my child. The nurse held me by the arm as I walked into the sunshine.

'There in the roadway was Charlie standing near the most beautiful car I had ever seen. He rushed towards me, and held my hands tightly, and said rather brokenly as he indicated the vehicle, "It is for you, darling."

'Back in our home the first room I visited was the nursery wherein all had been prepared for the child – the little cot and the rows of woolly toy animals.

'I sank down and covered my eyes with my hands, but not before I had seen the tears running down the cheeks of the little man with the blue, understanding eyes – the man whose mission in life was to make the world laugh and forget its pain.

'There were long days of illness for me and Charles knew of the ache in my heart. During those days of convalescence he was splendid. And for a while I occupied his thoughts to the exclusion of everything else. He and his great friend, Douglas Fairbanks, passed hours in my room, seeking to cheer my depression.

'And in that room, Charles would dance and prance about, mimicking anybody, joking, laughing; anything to raise my drooping spirits. He even donned the funny clothes with which all cinemagoers are familiar, the baggy trousers, the bowler hat, the comical little moustache.

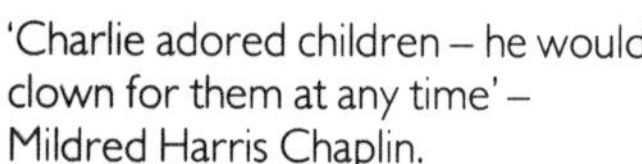
'Charlie adored children – he would clown for them at any time' – Mildred Harris Chaplin.

'Can you, in imagination, see that room? With Charles, his own heart full of sorrow, playing the jester so that my burden should be lightened. I believe his tremendous courage was born of the humbleness of his station in life when he was a boy.'

Commenting on the association of his personal tragedy and the making of *The Kid*, cinema historian Colin Frame wrote in 1957: '*The Kid* was released in the spring of 1921. It was Chaplin's longest film to date. Some still consider it his best. A year earlier, walking through the lobby of an hotel, he had seen a small boy curled up in a chair looking out on the world through big, solemn eyes. Chaplin had recently lost his boy, 'The Little Mouse' and something about this child tugged at his heart. He made inquiries and signed him up. And in *The Kid*, six-year-old Jackie Coogan became a star overnight.

'This was not the only autobiographical touch about the film,' Frame continued. 'There were others, pages from his early life, lifted out of the sordid and the ugly by the comic genius of Chaplin. All Chaplin's memories of the attics and alleys in Lambeth must have gone to the making of that film. And hardly noticed in this most brilliant of films, was an extra called Lita Grey. She was thirteen. In three more years she was to be the second Mrs Chaplin, and the mother of the sons he so dearly wanted . . .'

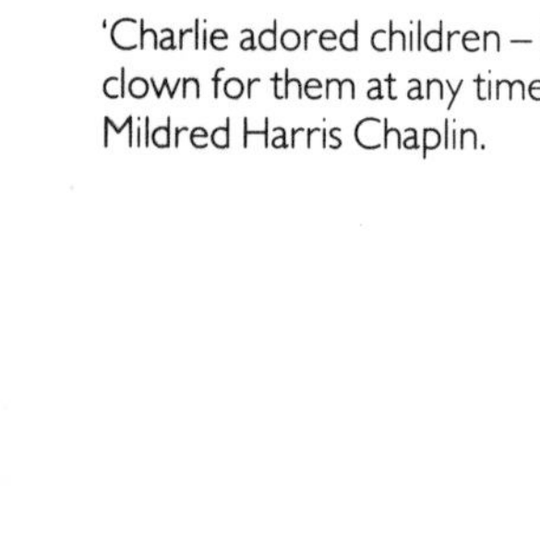

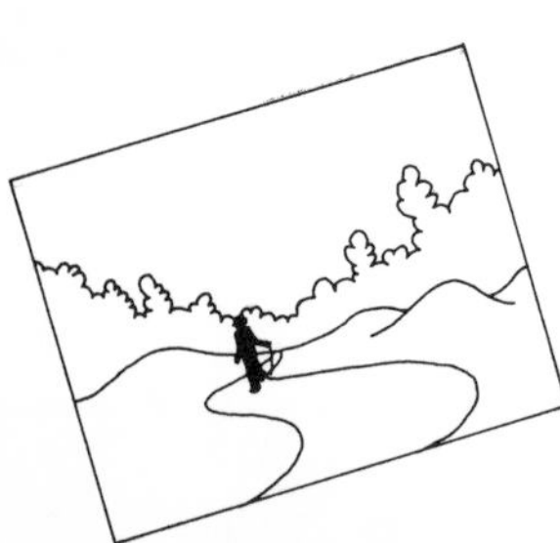

A JOURNEY BACK IN TIME

In September 1921, some eight years after he had sailed to America with the Fred Karno troupe and found fame and fortune, Charlie decided to make a return trip to England. Not surprisingly, he was accorded a hero's welcome when he arrived in London, having to appear on a balcony outside the Ritz Hotel to greet the thousands of fans who had gathered to see him. What he most wanted to do, though, was revisit the scenes of his childhood, and he finally managed to slip away unnoticed from the hotel in the company of three members of his entourage, the Scottish-born actor, Donald Crisp, script writer Tom Geraghty and Carlyle Robinson, the Press Representative he had appointed when setting up his own studio. Robinson was a former obituary writer in New York who had moved to Hollywood and after working for several movie studios, was offered a permanent job by Chaplin in 1917 which he held until 1932. On his return to Hollywood, Robinson gave the following description of Charlie's nostalgic visit to his roots:

'None of the invitations to tea and weekend house parties that Charlie received when he arrived in London really interested him. All he wanted to do was to roam about the haunts of his childhood and music hall days.

'The most memorable visit began one evening with a mysterious taxi drive on which Charlie invited Tom Geraghty, Donald Crisp and I to accompany him. Charlie whispered the instructions to the driver. We had no idea where he was taking us.

'After a while we found ourselves in the East End, and when the cab stopped we all got out. I could see the name of the place was Pownall Terrace. Charlie pointed out a tall, brick building that was one of a row set back about 50 feet from the pavement.

'His finger indicated what was obviously an attic room just below the sloping roof. "That's the room where I lived as a boy," he said. "I wonder if it's still the same?"

'Tom Geraghty said straightaway we should go up and find out. But Charlie was a bit reluctant. He did not want to embarrass the present occupant.

'I said I would go and make some inquiries. The others followed me into the hallway, which was in darkness, and then up the creaking stairs. Even the banisters squeaked. The topmost flight

was narrower than all the others, winding round in a semi-circle.

'When we got to the top landing it was so dark I lit a match and knocked on the only door I could see. After a brief wait, I heard the sound of a woman's voice asking who was there.

'"I am with Charlie Chaplin, who once lived here," I replied. "May we come in?"

'There was quite a delay before the door slowly opened. The occupant was obviously a bit suspicious about what I had said. And who could blame her!

'Inside, we saw a small room illuminated by an oil lamp, the glow from the wick casting a fitful light into the shadowy corners. We all had to stoop as we entered to avoid banging our heads on the slanting ceiling.

'At the far end of the room was a fireplace with some faintly glowing embers. On the hob was an iron kettle. A bed was pushed against the wall, its headboard jammed up against the low ceiling. Beside the bed was a straight-backed chair.

'The old woman who had let us in apologised for the humble surroundings, but Charlie's embarrassment was greater than hers.

'Little by little she unfolded her tale. Her name was Mrs Reynolds and she was a widow. Her husband had been killed in the war. She went across to the bed and brought out from underneath it an old tin box. From this she took out some pieces of paper and handed them to Charlie.

'"This is my husband's war record," she said, "and this is what he cherished most – a letter from the King."

'Charlie pretended to read the letter, but we knew he couldn't see what was written upon it. His eyes were misted by tears.

'When the woman suggested that we should all stay for a cup of tea, Charlie protested that it would be an imposition. But she would not take no for an answer.

'As she busied herself with the kettle on the iron hob, Charlie whispered to all of us to look for a knothole in a corner of the bare floor. We all searched about, but could find no trace of it. For the first time since we had entered the room, Charlie grinned.

'"It must have been plugged up," he said. "But when we lived here, Syd and I used to lie on our stomachs there and take turns at peeking at the people underneath!"

'When we finally left the room, the old woman begged us to call again. Charlie extended his hand. I remember the woman wiped her hands on her pinafore before shaking his. And as their hands met, there was the crackle of a bank note changing hands.

'We made our way back down the rickety stairs and out into the street. On the pavement, Charlie stopped and looked back up at the old building.

'"Well, boys" he said with what we could all tell was a lump in his throat, "you've been in the room where Syd and I clung on to life with our mother."'

On his return to Hollywood after visits to Paris and Berlin, Charlie wrote his own account of the trip, *My Wonderful Visit*, which was published in 1922. Although the book vividly records his nostalgia at re-visiting the scenes of his childhood, it strangely makes no mention of this moving experience in Pownall Terrace.

An evocative photograph of Charlie on the set he built in Hollywood to resemble the grimy, rubbish-strewn London streets in which he grew up.

I MET CHAPLIN IN THE NUDE!

Charlie followed the tremendous success of *The Kid* with several more inventive films including *The Pilgrim* (1923), *A Women In Paris* (1923) which he directed but only appeared in briefly as a station porter, and then the classic, *The Gold Rush*, in 1925. Other film makers were by now coming in increasing numbers to Hollywood to meet Chaplin and observe him at work, and among these was Anthony Asquith (the son of the former British Prime Minister, Lord Asquith) who in 1925 had helped found the English Film Society with H.G. Wells and George Bernard Shaw. Anthony went to Hollywood to learn the craft of film-making and then returned to England to carve out a distinguished career as a director which has subsequently inspired the much coveted annual Anthony Asquith Award for achievement in film music. He was introduced to the film world by Mary Pickford, who with her husband, Douglas Fairbanks, D.W. Griffith and Charlie Chaplin had recently formed United Artists, so a meeting with the great comedian was assured. How this came about in the winter of 1925 in what can only be described as the most unusual circumstances, he revealed in an article for the British magazine, *The Cine-Technician*. It was, though, to prove the beginning of a friendship that lasted until Asquith's death in 1968.

'I did not first meet Charlie Chaplin at Douglas and Mary's house as I had expected. Instead, it happened like this.

'Douglas was just then tidying up odd bits and pieces of *The Black Pirate* at the old United Artists Studio. At the end of every day, he would play a strenuous game of 'Doug,' a combination of lawn tennis and badminton which he had invented, then have a steam bath with his delightful trainer, Chuck Lewis, Al Parker (who was directing *The Black Pirate*), and any other friends who happened to be there. One evening, soon after the start of my visit, I arrived to watch the game. To see Douglas in action was an unforgettable experience. He combined agility and grace to a degree that I have hardly ever seen equalled. I was told he was already in the bath and I was now sufficiently one of the family to go straight in. Through the thick steam I could only see vague glistening outlines, but I could hear Douglas's voice. So, making a cautious detour round a large foreground piece, which proved to be Joe Schenk, I was about to announce my presence, when I

Anthony Asquith discussing films with Charlie during a visit to London.

was stopped by the sound of a new voice. Its owner was still swathed in a cocoon of steam. What arrested me was that, in spite of occasional superficial Americanisms of idiom and intonation, it spoke with what I had already come to regard as a strong English accent. It was a musical, cultivated voice with an occasional, indefinable whiff of cockney. I do not remember what he was saying but, looking back, it has always seemed to me paradoxical that my first personal impression of Charle Chaplin was purely aural and, when a moment later Douglas introduced me, my first feeling was surprise that he had a voice at all. I suppose I had assumed that someone whose every look and gesture conveyed his meaning so vividly and precisely, speech, with its clumsy ambiguity, must be not only unnecessary but a positive handicap.

It is not every day that you meet, for the first time, someone, for whose work you have an intense admiration, in the nude! But, there in front of me, still in soft focus and heavily gauzed by steam, stood one of the great artists of our time, wearing, as I was,

nothing but a loin-cloth. My own hands are not large, but the hand I now clasped seemed to evaporate into mine. Having only seen him in his screen make-up, I was not prepared for his distinguished good looks, but I think it was more the extraordinary mobility of feature than the features themselves that struck me. Watching Chaplin's face was like looking at a fascinating ballet or rather – for ballet implies something planned and formal – a spontaneous improvised dance.

With many people, the smile begins at the lips and reaches the eyes a second later. With some, it remains a meaningless muscular contortion confined to the lips only. Charlie's smile was essentially a smile of the eyes which did not necessarily need confirmation from his lips at all. It was largely the sense of immediate personal contact which his smile gave me and partly, no doubt, the dreamlike unreality of the setting that took away all shyness from me. I found myself talking to him as if I had known him for years. Charlie was a great talker in every sense of the word and his conversation in those days, at any rate, and I am speaking of nearly 30 years ago, was a curious mixture. He loved theorising about Art and Life, Religion and Politics, and, though what he said was always interesting, it was not unlike the conversation of a clever undergraduate. It was the kind of conversation I had been accustomed to at various literary or philosophical societies at Oxford, but, when he left Life in the abstract, and came to living people, it was a very different thing. I have never known anyone to compare with him in the power to make real and vivid a person he had met or an incident he had seen in the street. It was not a question of mimicry or verbal description, it was an act of creation. He, himself, disappeared, leaving a kind of ectoplasm from which the people, the setting, the event, materialised.

I met him often after this at Pickfair and at his own Studio, where he was still in the birth-pangs of *The Circus*. He and Mary were both, at that time, very excited by a film made on a shoestring by an unknown. It was called *The Salvation Hunters* and it was directed by Joseph Von Sternberg. They showed it to me and it was indeed a remarkable achievement. I had seen more German and Swedish films than they had, so I found its style and subject a little less startling than they did. Visually it was strikingly beautiful and Sternberg, like the Germans, had used the composition of the picture, the lighting and the camera angles just as much as the actors, to express the moods and emotions of the story.

I told Charlie afterwards I was surprised that he liked it so much because, during one of our talks, he had strongly disagreed with me about the merits of Dupont's *Vaudeville* which, though entirely different in subject, used the same kind of method. He had, for instance, disliked the way Dupont had identified the eyes of the spectator with that of his film characters at certain moments, particularly in a scene where a jealous trapeze artist, with murder in his heart, is swinging over the audience. Here, Dupont did not show the scene objectively, but put his camera on the trapeze, so that one had the feeling that one was, in fact, seeing through the eyes of the character concerned. Charlie thought this merely an irritating trick. To him, any odd camera angle, any composition of

a shot which was so striking as to draw attention to itself, was not expressive but merely a distraction. He maintained that such devices took the attention of the audience away from what was all-important – the doings and feelings of the people in the story.

Charlie always worked and played hard. Here seen on location near Lake Tahoe high in the Sierra Nevada mountains filming *The Gold Rush.*

I remember I argued that there might be moments when the emotions could, in fact, be better conveyed by the composition of the shot or the angle of the camera, that, for example, if someone in a story was terrified, you could help the actor by not only making him express terror with his face but by making what he saw look, in itself, terrifying. Of course, we were both right, but he was right about the really fundamental thing – the paramount importance of the human element. If you are not interested in the people, it does not matter how superficially exciting what happens to them may be, or indeed, how beautiful or

Charlie learning to fly with a friend in 1925.

arresting the pictures may be. You simply will not care. Charlie's imagination had been caught by the characters and theme of *The Salvation Hunters*, mine by its visual style.

In all Charlie's films, the people are the important thing and nowhere is that clearer than in the one film *A Woman of Paris*, which he directed but in which he did not appear. The greatest of all his creations, the screen figure of Charlie, is not there to monopolise our attention, but Chaplin, the Artist, is present in every foot. It is of particular interest because it is the one concrete embodiment of Charlie's conversation. I said that, when he described a person or an incident, he himself disappeared, leaving an ectoplasm out of which the person or event materialised. *A Woman of Paris*, apart from being a brilliant film, is of unique interest as being the only permanent record of this phenomenon.

Looking back, I realise now, far more than I did at the time, what a tremendous experience it was for me – a green, filmstruck undergraduate – to be able to talk for hours on end with the greatest artist the cinema has produced. Like every other really great man I have met, Charlie never talked down to anyone whom he felt was sincerely interested. It never occurred to me that it was colossal cheek for me to put forward my own unfledged ideas, to argue and even to disagree with him on his own subject. He never made you feel he was conferring a favour and so your immediate reaction was never – "how grateful I ought to be" but only – "what a wonderfully stimulating and exciting talk we (we!) have had." But, if I did not feel sufficiently grateful at the time, it was only a matter of delayed action. My gratitude has grown with the years at compound interest.

THE REASON FOR CHARLIE'S SILENCE

The year 1927 saw the arrival of the greatest development in films since moving pictures themselves had been invented – the advent of sound. The release of *The Jazz Singer* proved a milestone in cinema history, and while it certainly destroyed the careers of some silent stars whose voices proved totally ridiculous when heard on the screen, it opened a whole new world of sensations for movie audiences. Charlie, though, strongly resisted any suggestions that his Little Tramp should speak, and both his next two pictures, *City Lights* (1931) and *Modern Times* (1935) were silent, though both did have the addition of musical scores. Their undoubted box office success was the best answer to his critics, Charlie maintained. In December, 1930, when *City Lights* was being previewed around the world, he explained to an emigré English journalist, Charles Lapworth (one of the few Hollywood writers of the time he seemed to trust and allowed access to his studios) just *why* he was not going to speak.

'Why have I refused to talk in *City Lights*? I think the question really should be: Why *should* I talk? And if anyone insists that explanations are called for, why not ask those who at one fell swoop cut all the silent pictures out of the theatres. There were a lot of people who said they would like non-talkies as well as talkies. Were they listened to? Not very patiently. Talkies or nothing, they were told.

'When talkies were introduced a number of brave men gave ironclad reasons why talking pictures could never wholly satisfy, and I felt I had to take my place at their side. One by one they were won over. And some of them have acquitted themselves nobly with their new style pictures. But it left me rather lonely.

'I began to feel like the boy on the burning deck whence all but he had fled. I confess to some worry, but never to doubt. I wondered what the theatres would do about silent pictures when they would all be fitted out with 'babble machines' as H.G. Wells called them. The more I discussed the question with others, the more worried I got. Until I decided to go into a conference with myself. Then not only was there no doubt, but there was no worry either. I decided I would *not* talk!

'How did I arrive at that decision? Well, for one thing, in my mind, I ran over some of the old pictures, some of the outstanding episodes. And I tried and I tried to imagine and fit spoken words to those situations to see if I could have improved them. I knew I could not. My instinct, my whole being, is against resorting to words: and the more I thought about my past work the more was my instinct confirmed.

(Previous page) Charlie with Virginia Cherrill who played the blind flower seller in the poignant story of *City Lights* (1931).

'Only the curious would want to hear me speak, anyway. But millions want no change. Of that I am convinced. Their letters say that. And, strangely, the more talkies that come out, the more commands I get to keep silent!

'Pantomime is the oldest art, anyway. The good book says that in the beginning was the word, but people understood each other by signs before they did by sounds. And, I expect, understood each other better. Someone wrote that words were given us to conceal our thoughts. He anticipated the talkies. In some of the talkies

Although Charlie opposed the talkies, he believed 'music is divine' and scored his own pictures. In this rare photograph he is seen at work recording the sound track for *City Lights*.

the words are evidently used to demonstrate the absence of thought.

'Words can defeat the imagination. They destroy the illusion. People can be moved more intensely by a gesture than by a voice. I am not speaking of singing, of course. Singing is divine. I am speaking of the actor who has to speak. In an appeal to the emotions, the silent clown with his pantomime can beat the throaty tragedian every time.

'One of the strongest reasons why I should not talk is the fact that pantomime is the universal language. The Chinese children, the Japanese children, the Hindu, the African, all understand me. I doubt whether they would understand my Chinese or Hindustani. And if I were to be so crude as to give a thought to the commercial aspect, the whole world is still my market as long as I do not talk.

'Although I accept a lot of good work is being done in the talkie business, I think there is a chance that many of the pictures will not be so brilliant that they will keep human beings in whom tradition lingers from coming to see the old mimes and mummers.'

A NIGHT WITH THE WATER RATS

In 1931, Charlie undertook a world trip to promote *City Lights*, and for a second time returned to London, where he has reunited with a friend from his vaudeville days, the comedian, Wee Georgie Wood. The two men had first met in Oldham when appearing at separate theatres. Wee Georgie remembered that Chaplin had invited some of the boys and girls who were appearing in his show around for tea, but they had been prevented from going by their manager and Charlie had waited for them in vain for several hours. Never one to waste an experience, however, the star later utilised this episode to create a memorable scene in *The Gold Rush*. Wee Georgie, whom Charlie nick-named 'The Little Dynamo', had visited him in Hollywood in 1924, and was then the main instigator in conferring a special award on Chaplin when he came to London in February 1931. The tiny comic vividly recalled this occasion in an interview he gave in London in January 1956.

An intimate shot of Charlie on vacation in 1931.

272 PUNCH, OR THE LONDON CHARIVARI. [MARCH 11, 1931.

AT THE PICTURES.

CHARLIE AND "CITY LIGHTS."

CHARLIE (I will not say Mr. and I will not say CHARLES)—CHARLIE CHAPLIN is the Playboy of both hemispheres. No actor has ever had such a vogue, and, given the same conditions, it is doubtful if any other actor from the past could have equalled his popularity. GARRICK would have been too calculating, DAN LENO too simple. Nor, without the invention of the cinema, would CHARLIE, I think, have conquered. Always funny, it was for him and him alone, in his performance as the festive interrupter, that one used, years and years ago, to brave the rigours of the programmes of outlying music-halls where "KARNO'S Mumming Birds" were appearing; but one did not think of him then as ever to exceed in fame and in recognisable features all the great ones of the earth: kings, kaisers, prima-donnas and record-breakers in whatever branch of sport.

TRIUMPH OF THE TRAMP.
MR. CHARLES CHAPLIN.

Yet all the while it was only the camera that was needed. There was the man, with a brain fertile in comic invention, the impassive face ready for instantaneous mobility and light, the swift deft hands, the shuffling feet at an incredible angle; and no sooner was he photographed in action than the world knew what it had been waiting for. Since his films had no talking at all and the minimum of caption, and since they forswore all subtlety and their fabric was the rough humour of life wherever life is found, north or south, east or west, CHARLIE touched a universal chord. There was no need for translations or explanations; his gestures were themselves the best Volapuk, the best Esperanto. Hence Kamschatka knew him as closely as Kilburn, New Zealand as New York, Buenos Aires as Bordeaux. Hence his latest film, *City Lights*, which we have been expecting for so long and which was produced the other evening with so many circumstances of splendour, will evoke laughter in the remotest corners of the earth as well as in the Dominion Theatre.

The criticism may have a paradoxical sound, but *City Lights* is best when it is least funny. One goes to laugh and one does laugh, but the memorable moments are serious; that is to say, when the Tramp (CHARLIE) has provided the blind Flower-girl (Miss VIRGINIA CHERRILL), whom he adores, with enough money to undergo a healing treatment, and you then see across his features—features capable of abysmal melancholy—the doubt passing: "But, when she can see, won't she despise me?" There is no caption; the expression says all. And again at the very end, when, now seeing, she does not recognise him, and, although not despising, is not too friendly until her sense of touch on the hand that in her blind days used to reassure her brings gradually to her the knowledge that this ragged wastrel is her hero; while to him is brought at the same time the realisation that there is no contempt in her mind, but gratitude and love in her heart. On this discovery, silently but surely conveyed, the curtains unite.

STARRY LIGHTS.

There has been *en route* some glorious fooling, not least when CHARLIE swallows a whistle and becomes the involuntary invoker of cabs and dogs, and again when he enters the prize-ring and finds a real use for a referee. But the film is rather a series of episodes than a story and now and then is surprisingly unadventurous and not too well photographed. The scene, for instance, where the crooks are hiding in the background is feebly handled and indeed muddled; and we notice this the more because every other film that is now being shown has similar scenes capably and convincingly treated. CHARLIE'S momentary escapes are more ordinary than we should expect, and, although the effect was funny—as it always is and has been ever since films began—it seemed late in the day for jazz motor-driving, HAROLD LLOYD stuff, to be avoided by his predecessor and surpasser. It seemed to me too that now and then one of the original comic moments might have been extended, as when CHARLIE, like a new Laocoön, is in the toils of the macaroni and night-club coloured-paper streamers combined. Having stood up to reach to the swaying filament the better to swallow it, I think he might have climbed first on his chair and then on the table to be able to absorb still more. But it wouldn't surprise me if he knew best.

SPOTLIGHTS AT THE PREMIÈRE.
MR. BERNARD SHAW GETS A LITTLE.

It will be interesting to note how *City Lights* succeeds. CHARLIE is CHARLIE and must be seen; but it is a silent film and the present fashion is for talkies; it is a comic haphazard go-as-you-please film, and the present fashion is for emotion and plots. CHARLIE'S voice is pleasant and persuasive rather than vibrant, and some day he may give way and confide in the screen; but he will, I feel sure, if he does so, have to play different parts. It is not a voice for irresponsible and farcical antics; it would not go with

The world's most famous humour magazine, *Punch,* salutes the world's most famous comedy film star in words and cartoons when *City Lights* is premiered in London in March 1931.

'The night Charlie Chaplin became a member of the Grand Order of Water Rats was solemn and hilarious, moving and magnificently mad. In all my long association with this secret society of variety performers, in fact, I have never known the mood to change so swiftly. There were even a few nasty moments when the Rats smouldered on the verge of an anti-Chaplin riot!

'It all happened in 1931 – but it might never have taken place but for a chance meeting in Bud Flanagan's dressing room at the Victoria Palace. Bud, his partner, Chesney Allen, and Freddie and Charlie Austin, were playing cards when a famous head popped round the door and said to Charlie, "Hello, Oats!"

'It was Chaplin, using the Cockney rhyming slang he had never forgotten. "Oats" is short for "Oats and barley" – "Charlie". Freddie and Charlie were the younger brothers of Albert Austin who had gone to America with the same Fred Karno company as Charlie and later worked with him on many of his pictures.

'Charlie Austin was wearing his gold Water Rat emblem in his

lapel, and when Charlie saw it he sighed, "I used to yearn to be famous so that they would invite me to be a Rat."

'Well, after that it was agreed that Charlie Austin should propose Chaplin for membership and I, one of his closest friends in Britain, second him. Which brings me to the night in question.

'The initiation ceremony was due to start at eight o'clock on Sunday evening at our former headquarters in Old Compton Street, London. I've never seen such a turn-out of Rats – and every one of them arrived on the dot for a truly great occasion.

'In fact, the only person missing was Chaplin. There we sat, in our full regalia, waiting for the greatest man in show business, and getting more and more impatient.

'At nine o'clock, Charlie Austin, who was to escort him to the headquarters, rang up to say he was on his way, but had been delayed. The temper of the meeting improved a little.

'But by 10 o'clock the growls were well under way again. By 11 o'clock the temperature was even higher. In fact, had it not been for the efforts of Bud Flanagan, Chesney Allen and Clarkson Ross there might have been a mass walk-out.

'But these three saved the night – by bouncing in and out of the room every few minutes wearing Chaplin moustaches.

'Midnight came – and even the clowning of the trio was falling flat. Suddenly, the doors opened. And there, smiling uncertainly, stood a small, dapper figure.

'For a second there was silence. Then the entire audience, which a few minutes earlier had been about to stamp their feet, rose and cheered. The image of that Chaplin smile had swept away their anger. And the victory was complete when he explained that he had spent four hours battling his way to us. Not even the police had been able to clear a passage for him through the throngs trying to see him.

'A new Rat usually makes a solemn initiation speech. But there was never anything usual about Charlie! He gave us a full hour of spontaneous humour, impersonating great Water Rats of the past, giving his own wonderful impression – his 'party piece' – of a girl undressing in a French hotel!

'When it was all over, a crowd of us went on to Charlie Austin's flat for another hilarious party and finished up with Charlie at six in the morning somewhere in Kennington.

'"I feel I'd like to go back and see some of my old haunts again," Charlie said. So we joined him on this sentimental pilgrimage to the streets of his boyhood and early youth.

'But here I must confess something. The news of Chaplin's proposed initiation had spread round the West End like an epidemic. And when we took a count of the assembled members we found there were three more than there should have been.

'In the excitement and the melée, the Trap Guard and Test Rat, whose job it is to check the members on arrival, had failed to notice three gatecrashers.

'They were variety artists – but not Water Rats. And, as they had been present at the ceremony and had seen all our secret proceedings in the Lodge, there was only one thing left for us to do.

'So we did it. *We made them Water Rats!*'

A SOAKING FOR SUCCESS!

Charlie's second marriage in November 1924 to the 16-year-old Lita Grey who he had first noticed on the set of *The Kid*, resulted in two sons, Charles and Sydney, but not the happiness he sought, and the couple were acrimoniously divorced in August 1928. (Lita has since given her own rather sensationalised version of their marriage in *My Life With Chaplin, An Intimate Memoir*, 1966.) In 1932, Charlie met the woman who was to be his third wife, Paulette Goddard, a former Ziegfeld Follies dancer, who, when she heard that Chaplin was casting around for someone to play opposite him in *Modern Times*, clipped together some footage from her earlier pictures, showed it to the star, and got the part of the heroine. The picture was two years in the making, and at the end Charlie and Paulette were married. The marriage was short-lived and they parted in 1942. In 1972, when Paulette was living in Switzerland in a villa overlooking Lake Maggiore, not that far from where Chaplin himself had settled, she talked of how Charlie had made her 'the girl the world fell in love with' in *Modern Times*.

"Charlie changed a lot of things about me – from my shoes upwards!" Paulette Goddard, Charlie's co-star in *Modern Times* and his third wife.

Just one of the innumerable adaptations of the famous closing scene from *Modern Times* with Charlie and Paulette Goddard walking off into the sunset. This front cover of *Lilliput* was to mark Charlie's sixtieth birthday in 1949.

'Charlie changed a lot of things about me after we met. From the start he *understood* me. There is something in my character – *gamine* – the barefoot actress, and that was what he found.

'When I turned up to make *Modern Times* I was wearing the full glamour rig. Charlie took one look at me, shook his head, and said, "That's not it. That's *definitely* not it." He told me to take off my shoes, change my suit and remove my make-up. Then he threw a bucket of water all over me!

'The result was the hair style I've worn ever since. He also persuaded me to let my dyed blonde hair return to its natural colour – brunette with chestnut highlights.

'Then it was the clothes and the shoes. The thing is, most people look better with their shoes on. But me, without my shoes, I look, well, *grounded*! It's an animal quality that some people have found useful in me. Charlie made me take up ballet, too. I had this showgirl walk. I had to dump that in a hurry!

'During the two years it took to make *Modern Times*, Charlie encouraged me to take lessons in English literature, history, Spanish, French. When he wasn't filming, he was busy writing himself. He always wanted to be a writer, you know. He used to write a thousand words a day, and also study the Dictionary for at least an hour every day. He had no education, you see, and was desperate to learn.

'I suppose the scene I remember best from the actual shooting of the film was the part where Charlie and I spend the night in the department store and I wear a white ermine coat to keep warm. That was the first fur coat I had ever owned. I kept it after the film and used to tie an old handkerchief around the waist to make it look less like an ermine coat!

'*Modern Times* was really my school for acting. I think it's the best thing I ever did. Of course, it was before its time. People have developed enormously and really appreciate it today.

'When it first appeared in 1936 they gave it a society kick-off. You know the type of thing: with Elsa Maxwell and Mrs Hearst paying $50 a ticket. It was all wrong. Of course, they all hated the film! All those glossy capitalists watching the antics of a funny little man working in a factory. It was an artistic success, though, and after that everyone over-intellectualised Charlie's work and consequently he became self-conscious. It harmed him, I think.

'After making *Modern Times*, we got married and travelled for six months on Charlie's yacht – Bali, Indo-China, China, those sort of places. When we came back he was going to write another picture for me. But you know Charlie, it can take him forever!

'I guess he expected that a home, a Rolls Royce roadster, a swimming pool and a yacht ought to have satisfied me. We travelled some more. I studied psychology – I needed it – and rhetoric. But it wasn't enough. I was determined. I wanted to work.

'Mind you, I never took my career too seriously like some actresses. I was up for the role of Scarlett O'Hara in *Gone With the Wind* and Selznick had as good as decided on me. I gave a tennis party to celebrate and Laurence Olivier turned up with his girl friend, Vivien Leigh. Selznick took one look and that was that.

'Even after Charlie and I divorced we remained friends and sent

Paulette Goddard

Is She Your Choice For Scarlett O'Hara In . . .

GONE WITH the WIND

by MARGARET MITCHELL

Screen tests of Paulette Goddard for the role of Scarlett O'Hara have been successful, keeping her in the running for feminine lead in the movie version of "Gone With the Wind." During a long search, many important stars were considered for the part.

She Was a Chorus Girl. Blue-eyed, brown-haired Paulette Goddard (real name Pauline Levy) is 26, 4 feet, 4 inches tall, weighs 110 has been an actress for 10 years. Once a platinum blond chorus girl, she was on the stage in "Rio Rita" and George White's Scandals. In 1932 she was a showgirl in Eddie Cantor's film, "The Kid From Spain." She was born on Long Island, will have to learn green-eyed Scarlett O'Hara's Georgia drawl if she gets the coveted leading role in "Gone With the Wind."

Stepmother. Paulette, who married Charlie Chaplin on his yacht in 1934, enjoys the comradeship of his sons, Charles, 13, and Sydney, 12. Their mother is Lita Grey, Chaplin's second wife. He won a court fight to keep her from putting the boys in movies. He first wed Mildred Harris. His marriage to Miss Goddard has never been formally announced.

Page 30—Look—April 12, 1938

The third Mrs Chaplin might so easily have been Scarlett O'Hara as this report from *Look Magazine*, of April 1938, reveals.

Christmas cards to each other. We rarely met, though. I could understand why Charlie wanted to be left alone, why he didn't want to talk to the press. They always wanted to dig something up from the past – you know, "Whatever happened to Mildred Harris' first baby?", that kind of thing.

'Charlie once said that I was among the few people who understood him, but I didn't really. Still, he was right when he said one thing, "Every woman needs a man to discover her." I can vouch for that!'

THE SOUND OF TYRANNY

In the fullness of time Chaplin had to relent his decision not to make sound movies, and his last five pictures were all 'talkies': *The Great Dictator* (1940), *Monsieur Vedoux* (1947), *Limelight* (1952), *A King in New York* (1957) and *A Countess From Hong Kong* (1967). The Little Tramp, however, retained the silence for which he was famous, and although it can be argued there are elements of him to be found in Charlie's dual role of the Jewish barber and Adenoid Hynkel in *The Great Dictator*, there is little trace in the characters of the murderous Frenchman Vedoux, the fading comedian Calvero and the bewildered King Shadov. Among Charlie's entourage of associates at the time of this dramatic change in his style of film making was Rob Wagner, a former teacher of art who had joined Chaplin in 1919, briefly appeared before the cameras in *A Dog's Life*, and thereafter for many years helped orchestrate the maestro's publicity as well as writing a number of perceptive articles about him. Wagner was intimately involved in the creation of Chaplin's parody of Hitler, *The Great Dictator*, and reprinted the film's moving final speech in the

Charlie as the persecuted Jewish barber in *The Great Dictator* (1940).

As the murderous Frenchman, *Monsieur Verdoux* (1947).

Charlie portraying Calvero, the fading comedian, in *Limelight* (1952).

November 1940 issue of a Hollywood-based magazine he edited, *Script*. Two years earlier, in January 1938, Wagner printed an item entitled 'Rhythm – A Story of Men in Macabre Movement' about the execution of a brilliant Spanish humourist which was stated to have been written by Charles Chaplin. How much Wagner had been involved in the writing of this story is difficult to judge – his hand is certainly evident in a number of other articles credited to Chaplin during this period – but there seems little doubt that it was a forerunner of the ideas Charlie was to develop in *The Great Dictator* and is reprinted as a unique piece of Chaplin memorabilia.

RHYTHM
A Story of Men in Macabre Movement

Charles Chaplin

Only the dawn moved in the stillness of that small prison yard – the dawn ushering in death, as the young Loyalist stood facing the firing squad. The preliminaries were over. The small group of officials had stepped to one side to witness the end and now the scene had tightened into ominous silence.

Up to the last, the Rebels had hoped that a reprieve would come from Headquarters, for although the condemned man was an enemy to their cause, in the past he had been a popular figure in Spain, a brilliant writer of humour, who had contributed much to the enjoyment of his fellow countrymen.

The officer in charge of the firing squad knew him personally. Before the civil war they had been friends. Together they had been graduated from the university in Madrid. Together they had worked for the overthrow of the monarchy and the power of the Church. And together, they had caroused, had sat at nights around café tables, had laughed and joked, had enjoyed evenings of metaphysical discussion. At times they had argued on the dialectics of

government. Their technical differences were friendly then, but now those differences had wrought misery and upheaval all over Spain, and had brought his friend to die by the firing squad.

But why think of the past? Why reason? Since the civil war, what good was reason? In the silence of the prison yard these interrogative thoughts ran feverishly through the officer's mind.

No. He must shut out the past. Only the future mattered. A world in which he would be deprived of many old friends.

That morning was the first time they had met since the war. But no word was spoken. Only a faint smile of recognition passed between them as they prepared for the march into the prison yard.

From the sombre dawn streaks of silver and red peered over the prison wall, and breathed a quiet requiem in rhythm with the stillness in the yard, a rhythm pulsating in silence like the throbbing of a heart. Out of that silence the voice of the commanding officer resounded against the prison walls. 'Attention!'

At this command, six subordinates snapped their rifles to their sides and stiffened. The unity of their action was followed by a pause in which the next command was to be given.

But in that pause something happened, something that broke the line of rhythm. The condemned man coughed and cleared his throat. This interruption broke the concatenation of procedure.

The officer turned, expecting the prisoner to speak, but no words came. Turning to his men again, he was about to proceed with the next command, but a sudden revolt took possession of his brain, a psychic amnesia that left his mind a blank. He stood bewildered before his men. What was the matter? The scene in the prison yard had no meaning. He saw only objectively – a man with his back to the wall facing six others. And the group there on the side, how foolish they looked, like rows of clocks that had suddenly stopped ticking. No one moved. Nothing made sense. Something was wrong. It must all be a dream, and he must snap out of it.

Dimly his memory began to return. How long had he been standing there? What had happened? Ah, yes! He had issued an order. But what order came next?

Following 'Attention!' was the command 'Present arms' and after that, 'To aim', and then 'Fire!' A faint concept of this was in the back of his mind. But words to utter it seemed far off – vague and outside of himself.

In this dilemma he shouted incoherently, jumbled words that had no meaning. But to his relief the men presented arms. The rhythm of their action set his brain in rhythm, and again he shouted. Now the men took aim.

But in the pause that followed, there came into the prison yard hurrying footsteps, the nature of which the officer knew meant a reprieve. Instantly, his mind cleared. 'Stop!' he screamed frantically at the firing squad.

Six men stood poised with rifles. Six men were caught in rhythm. Six men when they heard the scream to stop – fired.

DICKENS AND CHAPLIN: THE UNIVERSAL ARTISTS

Investigating Charlie Chaplin's life brings to light a number of fascinating parallels with another famous Englishman, one of the nation's greatest writers, Charles Dickens. Indeed, Charlie made several references to the immortal author during his life and was, of course, born into the same kind of impoverished background that Dickens so vividly described in his works. This said, it hardly comes as too much of a surprise to learn that the little man nursed a tremendous admiration for the literary giant who had died only a matter of a few years before he was born.

'It was still the London of Dickens' Charlie commented about his humble birthplace in his autobiography: a point Colin Frame underlined in a revealing article he wrote for *The Star* newspaper in 1952. 'This was Victorian London,' he wrote, 'but not the London of the Gaiety and the Gay Nineties. It was more the London of Fagin and the Artful Dodger and Oliver Twist. Charles Dickens died 19 years before Charles Chaplin was born, but many of the scenes of which he had written with such knowledge and compassion were still found in darker London.

'And it cannot be sheer concidence,' Frame went on, 'that Chaplin films have always shown a broad humour, with the poor and destitute as heroes, humanity and compassion, sympathy for the underdog and an underlying message of revolt against a system. Many people have observed the likeness between the two Charleses. Chaplin influenced by his early environment used the camera to tell the sort of stories Dickens would have loved.'

Charles Dickens – whose work was inextricably linked with that of Chaplin.

Among these 'many people' that Colin Frame mentions can be listed the distinguished British novelist and poet, L.A.G. Strong who called Charlie 'the most complete Dickensian of our time'. Speaking in 1951, he said: 'That coincidence of pathos and force, that black and white over-simplified view of the antagonists in our human scene, the very outlook on life – you will see them in every one of Chaplin's own films, and, best of all, in his first serious picture, *A Woman of Paris*, which is Dickens undisguised. This genius of the Twentieth Century we owe to that genius of the Nineteenth. And Charlie's accomplishment takes us straight to the other great Dickens' legacy – pantomime.' His words have been reinforced by Professor W.W. Robson of Oxford University who said in 1969, 'Dickens' art is like Chaplin's: as universal and as great.' And film critic Peter Cotes has the last word: 'Chaplin is

BIRKENHEAD
HIPPODROME
Sole Proprietor ... ... D. J. CLARKE
This Theatre is booked in conjunction with Argyle Theatre, Birkenhead. Palladium Theatre, Southport. Theatre Royal, Hippodrome and Winter Gardens, Dublin. Royal Hippodrome, Belfast. Hippodrome, St. Helens

Programme.

MONDAY NEXT
Bransby Williams
and his own Selected Company
IN A SERIES OF
DICKENS' PLAYS

Monday, May 16 ... DAVID COPPERFIELD
ALSO
Monday, May 23 ... The Renowned Dramatic Play THE RED LAMP

PRICES OF ADMISSION:

	Private Boxes	Orchestra Stalls	Dress Circle	Grand Circle	Stalls	Pit Stalls	Pit	Family Circle
SINGLE SEAT	7/6	5/-	5/-	3/6	4/-	3/-	2/-	1/6

All Seats bookable in advance.
All the above prices are subject to the Entertainment Tax.
Telephone—B'head 600
Box Office open from 10 a.m. to 9-30 p.m.
B. Haram & Co., "Advertiser" Office, Hamilton Street, Birkenhead.

A programme for Bransby Williams, the actor who inspired Charlie's love of Dickens.

the Dickens of the film world, with a dash of Shakespeare's ardour, poetry and universal significance.'

It is quite true, in fact, that a number of Dickens' characters can be seen thinly disguised in Chaplin's films: Jo, the crossing sweeper, for instance, and Oliver Twist and Smike are surely blood brothers of the Kid; while the likes of Dora, little Nell, Florence Dombey and Emily all appear in picture after picture.

A number of sources have noted that Charlie read and re-read the Dickens' novels – journalist Margaret Laing, for instance, who met the little man on a fishing holiday in Ireland in 1964, was told by him, 'The only author I read for pleasure is Dickens.' Chaplin's children, too, have confirmed how familiar their father was with the novelist's stories. Writing in his book, *My Father, Charles Chaplin*, the eldest, Charles Chaplin jnr said in 1960:

'Dad, like a good father, always told us bedtime stories. But what stories! Sometimes they would be ghost stories and Syd and I would lie there listening, feeling a thrill of delightful fear. Often his stories came from Dickens, but there were not, as you might expect, the sentimental or mildly satirical passages with which Dickens abounds. They were those which had a macabre cast to

them. Oddly enough, my father and Dickens were alike in their predilection for the macabre.'

Charlie junior has also provided us with an evocative description of his father's bedtime story sessions which is so delightful as to make anyone wish they had been there: 'I think Oliver Twist was a favourite of Dad's because young Oliver's experiences in the orphanage so closely approximated his own. The passage he usually chose to act out for us is the one that describes Oliver Twist's meeting with Fagin.

"How'd you like to be the little boy just waking up and you see this man with a beard standing there and the knife coming at you?' he would say in that soft, forebidding tone of voice that always ushered us into one of his characterisations. Then contorting his face, he would begin playing the part of Fagin, hissing

'"What do you watch me for? Why are you awake? What have you seen? Speak out, boy! Quick-quick! For your *life*!"

'Dad repeated the story often, but I don't recall his ever telling it in the same way. Each time he would add fresh embellishments from his own imagination, so that Syd and I never knew exactly what to expect. But we could always count on its being exciting!'

Charlie's undoubted fascination with Dickens caused him to make an exception to his rule of never giving after dinner speeches and accept an invitation from the Dickens' Fellowship to be their guest of honour in London on February 7, 1955 to mark the 143rd anniversary of the great writer's birth. Over 300 members crowded into the Café Royale for the rare privilege of hearing the cinema star talking about Dickens' influence upon him – and how it came about.

Although the speech was referred to in the British national newspapers the following morning, it has never been reprinted in full in a book. It makes fascinating reading not only for it's insight into the beginnings of Chaplin's admiration for Dicken's, but more specifically for some views about the state of the world he believed both of them would have shared. Welcomed by the President of the Society, Earl Jowitt, as 'the greatest artist that the

Self-portraits of Bransby Williams and Charlie Chaplin from the author's collection of caricatures.

Charlie also revealed his horror of weapons in *The Great Dictator*, from which this amusing still is taken!

screen has produced and, I believe, one of the immortals,' Charlie began his own tribute in typically light-hearted fashion . . .

'After such a compliment, I am reminded of the story of the widow and her little boy attending the funeral of her husband. The minister was extolling his virtues, saying what a wonderful man he was, what a kind and generous father, what a home-loving, family man. The widow turned to her little boy and said, "Son, I think we have come to the wrong funeral!"

'I am very happy to have the honour of proposing the toast to the Immortal Memory of that great master of letters Charles Dickens. There is somebody whom I wish were here tonight, because he was a man who was responsible for inspiring, and I should say, enlivening, a young boy's interest in literature.

'I remember, at the age of eight, when I was with the Eight Lancashire Lads, a troupe of clog dancers, standing in the wings of the Empire Music Hall, Glasgow, and I stood there enthralled, as I watched a world for the first time, a new world of romance, mystery and wonderment, enacted by a very handsome gentleman imitating characters from Charles Dickens. The memory of those moments in the wings has left an indelible impression upon me.

'The gentleman responsible for those moments was Mr Bransby Williams. I am truly sorry that he is not here tonight. For he is one of the few persons I can say I remember when I was a little boy!

'I used to imitate Bransby Williams's characters from Charles Dickens – in particular the old man from *The Old Curiosity Shop*. The manager of the theatre saw me and said, "This must be given to the people!" Adding (he was so enthusiastic about my performance), "You must appear at the Empire in Middlesborough."

'I remember the man made a very impassioned speech about the young genius of eight years of age who was going to do the old man from *The Old Curiosity Shop*, who could not recognise death in his little grand-daughter. They bought me a cheap wig with strands of ragged grey hair. I was somewhat small for my age and this very large wig fell about my ears!

'Anyhow, I came on bent – I must have looked more like a Martian beetle than the old man of the curiosity shop! I went on stage and in a voice which could not be heard over the footlights, I remember saying: "Ssh! You must not make a noise or else you will wake my Nellie!"

'And someone in the audience shouted, "Louder!" – and that was the end of my history on the stage! But it was only the beginning of my discovery of the marvellous worlds to be found in Dickens' stories.

'I would venture to say that if Charles Dickens were alive today, he would be critical of our time. He would be critical about our Western Democracy which, in my humble opinion, is not without its hypocracy and double talk; wanting peace and, at the same time, urging a race for armaments, with promises of more blood, sweat and tears.

'Dickens would, I am sure, have been critical of the Cold War, because it has achieved nothing, has not determined anything, other than to make the whole world neurotic and to give a powerless feeling to our young people. Hate, suspicion and fear are bad things to have in these days of nuclear inventions and the horror weapons.

'Therefore, I say, I think he would have written eloquently about this matter. He would have been critical of the scientists, of the lack of moral responsibility in handing over the atomic bomb to the military. The mere conception of it is a black mark against the human race. It we are to survive in this day of nuclear energy and these weapons of destruction, we must develop something more than cleverness; we must develop tolerance and kindness for our fellow men.

'It is not enough to be intellectual, we must have feeling; criminologists tell us that intellect and no feeling can be ascribed to the arch-criminals, the Nazis, the Goerings and the Hitlers.

'In considering a balance of both feeling and intellect in proportion, we can survive, and we can make of this, the nuclear age, a grand and glorious adventure for us all. It was this beautiful balance of intellect and feeling that was the soul of Dickens; it was the essense of his work which he gave to the world.

'His literary work has added much to the greatness of English letters and to the greatness of England itself. To that greatness I do, with very sincere admiration and love, raise my glass to the undying memory of our beloved Charles Dickens!'

LEADING LADY TO THE KING

The last picture in which Charlie Chaplin was to star was *A King in New York* which he made in 1956 in his native England at Shepperton Studios – following his exile from America as a result of the now notorious campaign of vilification averring that he was a Communist sympathiser. (In his only other subsequent picture, *A Countess From Hong Kong* which he shot in 1966, he just appeared briefly as an old steward.) It was perhaps fitting that he should have made the story of King Shadov close to his roots in London, and that in picking a co-star, Dawn Addams, he selected a pretty young actress who had been born in Felixstowe, Suffolk!

Charlie had actually first seen Dawn working in Hollywood on *The Moon is Blue* in 1953 and almost signed her for *Limelight*. Instead, she was offered what proved the plumb role of her career as the young advertising executive, Ann Kay, and in September 1957 when the picture was released, revealed what it was like working with the legendary star. Of particular interest are her comments about Charlie insisting on her keeping her head still

Dawn Addams, the Suffolk-born actress who appeared in Charlie's last starring picture, *A King in New York* (1956).

while acting – the very first lesson he *himself* had learned half a century earlier from his mentor, H.A. Saintsbury . . .

'I first met Charlie in the winter of 1955 when he invited me and my husband to his home at Vevey in Switzerland. He met us on the snow-covered platform of the local station, and before we had reached his house he had told me half the story of the film, illustrating everything with his own incomparable gestures!

'The next day he acted the whole script for me and then made me read a scene with him. When I left Vevey, he dumped the script in my hands and said, "I won't make the picture without you." That was a tremendous relief as I was terrified at the thought of having to do a film test. I knew I would muff it. He understood this and said it wouldn't be necessary.

'When work on the film actually began at Shepperton, the first scene we read together was one of the opening scenes from the picture – and, I think, one of the funniest. Charlie as the exiled King was flirting with me all through this dinner party and I was responding. But though he thought I was interested in him as a man, I was only interested in him at that time from a professional point of view.

'Well, he walked through my scene for me. But at one point he stepped over the chalk line on the studio floor which indicated the limit of the camera's range. Spontaneously, I exclaimed, "But Mr Chaplin, you're over your mark." There was a horrible moment of silence which everyone held their breath. I thought, "Oh, goodness, what have I said? And on the first day, too."

'Then Charlie roared with laughter. Everyone joined in. The tension was broken and after that we all worked in a much more relaxed atmosphere.

'I learned so much from Chaplin about acting. He believes in simplicity. "Break through" was his favourite instruction. He wanted us to find the happy medium between ourselves and our roles. I had never had such tuition in playing a film part before.

'Another thing he taught me was not to nod my head when I was acting. This infuriated him. "Remember to be definite," he said, "moving your head is indefinite. Only make a move when it means something."

'There was one scene I could not get right. It was between Charlie and I in my hotel room. Charlie tried hard to help me "break through", but I just couldn't make it. I don't know whether the fault was mine or the script. But Charlie understood and changed the order of the dialogue.

'Shooting that scene took a whole day and afterwards I felt terrible about it. But when I tried to apologise he only laughed. "Once with Paulette (Goddard) it took four days to get a scene right," was his only comment.

'Another thing that was very helpful was that Charlie liked to shoot scenes in sequence as much as possible. As the producer, that was something he could decide.

'I enjoyed every minute of watching Chaplin rehearsing his own part, and in fact I used to go to the set every day even when I was not working, not wanting to miss a single moment of him at work.

Charlie made a fleeting appearance as an old steward in what was to be his final movie, *A Countess from Hong Kong* (1967). This sketch of the picture's stars, Sophia Loren and Marlon Brando, by the cartoonist Ffolkes appeared in *Punch*, January 18, 1967.

'Although he had worked out most of his own gags beforehand, he still kept on improvising and changing things until he was satisfied. When he fumbled a line or seemed unsure of a scene, he would usually have indigestion over lunch!

'I remember that once during rehearsals when I didn't seem too sure of my lines, he asked, "Do you know your lines?" Before I could reply he added, "I don't know mine, but as I wrote them it doesn't matter. I have an excuse because I have to keep my eye on everything. You're a young thing, you don't want me to be better than you, surely?"

'As far as new screen techniques were concerned, Charlie was worried about being old fashioned. The man who had made what was comparatively speaking a silent picture eight years after talkies had become the craze, was equally unenthusiastic about the bigger screens.

'It was four years since he had made *Limelight* and the new techniques still bothered him. He couldn't believe they would last – and knowing that his film stood a good chance of doing so, he did not want to commit it to some fly-by-night technical discovery. He thought of using colour, but chose to stick to black and white. His one concession was accepting the panoramic screen process.

'This caused him a good deal of problems. Every now and then the cameraman would say that the frame had to be narrower. At this, Charlie would yell, "But I can't have a hotel room that shape! I want air for my people." He'd then look through the lens and see how the picture would appear on the Cinemascope screen and tear his hair. It was obviously frustrating for him to have to see a scene in two different sizes!

'Some of his old techniques did not change at all. For example, for the smaller parts in the film he chose variety artists as they could do the gags as he wanted them done. But it can never be easy for any actor or actress to execute exactly what Chaplin has shown he wants. For the truth is, he can play every part in a film so much better than any of us!

'Charlie was really rather like a musical conductor when he directed. Sometimes he was suddenly a saxophone or a violin to give us the mood of the scene. He understands music so well that he harmonises a scene according to a musical criterion. He watches for the key theme and then leads it up to a crescendo.

'Timing film comedy is so different from what is used on the stage – and I learned for the first time the importance of putting a bit-of-nonsense after a big laugh so that dialogue is not lost on the audience. Undoubtedly working with the "King" of comedy was one of the most demanding and rewarding experiences of my life.'

THE FORGOTTEN FRIENDS

When Charlie published his long awaited work, *My Autobiography*, in 1964, his millions of admirers and colleagues hoped that the star's own words would at last set right all the rumours, half-truths, even lies, that had been written and spoken about him and his career over the years. Though the book was undeniably a fascinating history, rich in details of his childhood and full of information about his colourful public life, there were a good many people and places that were either sketched over or totally omitted. Only those who had been close to Charlie knew the facts about these periods, and a considerable number of these

Robert Florey, Charlie's friend, who was so dismayed by the ommissions from the star's Autobiography.

were now dead. So who was there to comment on the omissions that experts knew were there and for a variety of reasons Charlie had decided to gloss over? One of the star's closest colleagues for many of his Hollywood years was Robert Florey, a French-born cinema enthusiast who had come to the film capital in 1921 to write about the stars and remained to become a leading director. He also became an intimate friend of Chaplin and many of the other leading directors of the time like Josef von Sternberg and King Vidor. In 1947, Chaplin paid him the ultimate compliment of appointing him associate director on *Monsieur Vedoux*. Florey naturally read Charlie's book with more than usual interest – not to mention a mounting sense of frustration – and in December 1964 wrote for *Cinemonde* magazine what is perhaps *the* insider's view of the work. This is the article's first appearance in English and it provides an interesting counterpoint to some of the views expressed in this book. Some years before his death in 1979, Florey's contribution to the cinema was marked by the French government who made him a Knight of the Legion d'Honneur.

'There is much that I have found disappointing in Charlie Chaplin's autobiography. For example, I was disappointed not to find in the chapter dealing with his arrival in Hollywood a more detailed description of the rising cinema industry – of a world that was so picturesque then, when one saw taxi drivers and out-of-work girls become stars overnight; hairdressers change into directors and butchers set up as producers!

'I found the book tends to give the impression that Charlie led a very fashionable existence which he interrupted – occasionally – to make films. He writes that it was he himself when under contract by Mack Sennett who had the idea of the tramp's outfit. Maybe. But that does not correspond with the accounts given to me by the stars of Keystone – Chester Conklin, Roscoe 'Fatty' Arbuckle and Ford Sterling. These men assured me that they helped in his 'transformation': Chester lending Charlie his boots, Arbuckle a hat and his trousers, and Sterling the moustache. Besides which, for some time the comedian Billy Ritchie had been appearing on the stage dressed almost exactly the same!

'Charlie is so preoccupied with the fear of forgetting – if only for a moment – the great people of the world whom he has met in the course of half a century, that he loses track of marvellous comrades, of collaborators, and some of his most devoted admirers. He breathes not a word about one of his most famous films, *The Circus*, but makes a point of informing us that the ex-Queen of Spain is his neighbour. He describes at length his meetings with Churchill, the Prince of Wales, Chou En-lai, Gandhi, Princess Margaret, Franklin Roosevelt, etc. But only once does he mention, by his first name, his faithful cameraman, Rollie Totheroh, who, with Henry Bergman, Alfred Reeves, Leo White, Eric Campbell and Harry Crocker, were among his most constant collaborators. Bergman worked for more than 25 years with Chaplin, until after *The Great Dictator*.

With regard to more personal events we find the same strange omissions. From 1915 to 1922, the charming Edna Purviance was

A dramatic moment in the lion's cage from *The Circus* (1928) which Robert Florey considered Charlie's best picture – though the star never mentioned it in his book.

his partner in 34 films. But, writing of *A Woman of Paris*, in which he directed her, he says that the film made Adolphe Menjou a star, but that Edna 'did not quite make the grade'. He adds that the actress left for Italy to make a film which was not a success and that was the end of her career. As he was busy making films with Georgia Hale, Merna Kennedy, Virginia Cherrill, Paulette Goddard and others, Charlie did not see Edna again for some 20 years.

'He also skips over another fact of which the historians of cinema history would love an explanation. After *A Woman of Paris*, Edna Purviance was the star of a film directed by Josef von Sternberg, which Chaplin was well aware of as he was the producer and also a partner. *The Seagull* (also known as *A Woman of the Sea*) was filmed in his studio at La Brea, on location at Monterey, and photographed by Paul Ivano. After seeing the first run-through, Chaplin had a large part of it re-filmed.

'I was actually at the preview in the Dome Theatre in Beverley Hills. Like all von Sternberg's films it was brilliantly directed. Edna showed undeniable qualities, being very different from the automatom of *A Woman of Paris* as she had not been ordered to distort her movements and expressions. Yet, this film was never released.

'Chaplin had not been present at the preview and it was said that as von Sternberg had held this without informing him, Charlie had decided not to release the picture. *The Seagull* had cost a lot of money, and for its producer to decide to lose such a large sum of dollars there must have been an important reason. I had hoped to find it in his book. In vain! If the film had been inferior, if Edna had been mediocre, if the quality of the production had not been up to normal standards, Chaplin's decision would have been understandable, but *The Seagull* was a fine work and well in advance of the cinema standards of the time – Josef von Sternberg not being just anybody! It was only after this event that Edna Purviance's career came to an end. The release of the film, without a doubt, would have changed her future.

'During the next 20 years Chaplin did not once see his old friend. I met her occasionally. She never complained, hoping to appear again with the man she had loved. In fact, she saw him just once more. In 1946 we did a film test of Edna for *Monsieur Vedoux*. Her face had hardly changed, the same pretty smile lit up her features, and she had lost none of her charm and sweetness.

'Chaplin rehearsed her, but told her she was not right for the part. Afterwards, I walked across the studio yard with her. There were tears in her eyes, knowing that she would never come back. I kissed her and promised to call her soon.

'Returning to the stage, I met old Henry Bergman who asked me if there was a small part for him in the film. I thought of the part of the judge who doesn't speak a word while he listens to the interminable tirade of the criminal, but Chaplin refused. So I had to send away the fat man who had appeared in all Charlie's films over the years, and of whom he had once declared that his presence, even silent in a corner, brought luck to a production. Bergman died, forgotten, a few weeks later.

Another charming man who can be placed at the top of the list of 'forgotten ones' is Charlie's half-brother, Wheeler Dryden.

(Opposite page) Edna Purviance, who Robert Florey claims was badly treated by Chaplin, in a scene from *By The Sea* made in 1915.

A sad little item about Henry Bergman, another of the people Chaplin forgot. From *The Film Weekly*, November 1, 1930.

Charlie Chaplin, who pays a £15 a week pension to his best yes-man

The World's Best YES-MAN

by MICHAEL MOORE

HENRY BERGMAN, proprietor of "Henry's," Hollywood's undeservedly popular restaurant, is the world's best yes-man. He earns £150 a week from his restaurant and £15 a week for yessing.

The £15 is a pension from Charlie Chaplin, who originally financed the restaurant. Ever since anyone can remember, Charlie has paid Henry £15 a week. He plays as an extra in every Chaplin picture. He attends every Chaplin conference and sits with his little eyes glued on Chaplin's face. Long practice has enabled him to anticipate the comedian's every reaction. If a suggestion appeals to Charlie, Henry says so first; if Charlie doesn't like it, Henry, gifted beyond his fellows in subsidised telepathy, beats him to it with: "That's terrible, isn't it?"

Not long ago Henry was forgotten. His £15 continued to arrive each week—but no one asked him to report at the studio. Stricken like a deserted bride, the fat little restaurateur retired to his ranch in the San Fernando Valley, just beyond the range of hills which prevents Hollywood from infecting civilisation to the north and north-west.

For a Month He Languished

For a month he languished there, with no one to look after him except the man who feeds the pigs. For hours every day he would sit near the roadside watching every car that passed, expecting each one to contain Chaplin, come to summon him to a conference.

In one month he lost forty pounds in weight. His celebrated *embonpoint* shrank like the kernel of a set of orphaned bag-pipes. His cheeks became hollow and his eyes dim.

At last someone heard of his condition and told Chaplin.

"What the hell?" said Chaplin. "Send for him."

"What's the matter with you?" he said when Henry arrived. Henry gazed at him with dumb reproach. Charlie took him by the arm and led him to his bungalow, sat him in a chair, draped a towel round him and cut his hair. Neither of them spoke.

"There," said Charlie, surveying his handiwork. "Now go away to Catalina (an island resort near Los Angeles), have two weeks' holiday, come back and—and help me."

Henry beamed and went. In two weeks he was back, fatter than ever, glistening with hero-worship and avoirdupois, yessing like a steam engine.

Can friendship go further?

Actor, stage-manager, producer, secretary, wardrobe keeper, responsible for getting food for his famous relative, dusting his possessions, drudge and scapegoat, constantly being reprimanded without ever protesting. Dryden worshipped Charlie, followed him on the set at a respectful distance, keeping off intruders, carrying his scenarios and even several pairs of spectacles for Charlie who was forever mislaying them! Wheeler also took care that the artist's meditations were not interrupted and gave him his cues whenever he wanted to rehearse his lines: modest, quiet and self-effacing, he never took time off to rest.

'But all this self-denial, devotion and patience did Wheeler no good. He is no longer with us, and no trace of him is found in the memoirs of his half-brother. I have likewise searched in vain for the names of Monta Bell, Harry d'Abbadie d'Arrast, Eddie Sutherland and Jean de Limur who all became producers but whom he avoids mentioning.

'Among those who were his friends and of whom he tells us nothing, we must also mention, Max Linder whom he called his "teacher" and with whom he often dined and went out with to boxing matches in Vernon and motor racing in Culver City; Sadakichi Hartman, an actor with a strange face, whose mother

was Japanese and father German; Jim Tully, an Irish red-head, novelist, poet, boxer and hobo; George Jomier, the oldest Frenchman in Hollywood, gourmet, good fellow, teacher, connoiseur of wine, who cooked up special dishes for Chaplin at Max Linder's place; Carter de Haven, a former star, musician, producer and impresario; Charles Reisner, actor, gagman, producer and stage manager, the father of Dinky Dean whom Chaplin hoped to turn into a second Jackie Coogan; Eddie Manson, a publicist who followed Carlyle Robinson; Big Bill Tilden, the tennis champion who gave Charlie lessons; Mabel Smith, who predicted regularly – but not infallibly – the future; John Decker, the painter and caricaturist; Frank Testera, chief electrician and stage setter on whose co-operation Chaplin could always count; King Vidor, who was to be seen so often in the restaurants of Beverley Hills with Charlie; and Albert Austin and Stan Laurel, his friends from Karno days, whom he just mentions vaguely.

'Charlie shows no gallantry towards the women who loved him. Oh, no! Talking of his first wife, Mildred Harris, a very pretty girl of 18, he tells us that she did all the running. He did not love her, his only interest in her being purely sexual, and that it would have been too much of an effort for him, apparently, to act as the passionate lover! He confided to Douglas Fairbanks that Mildred was not an "intellectual giant". It is true that after many dinners, dances and nightly walks Mildred became pregnant and Chaplin was obliged to marry her. She was not yet twenty when they separated – "irreconcilably unsuited". Chaplin found his wife exasperatingly femine, with "a mind encumbered with stupid ideas tied up in pink ribbon"!

'I directed Mildred Harris in the silent days. She was not without spirit, but calm, pleasant, always listening carefully to advice. She played comedy easily, was ready on time, and never put on the airs of many female stars. Her talent, in fact, was all that one could ask from an artiste in those days.

'I remember we were filming in Pasadena once, and she spoke of her ex-husband. There was no bitterness. "It is hard for a girl to be the wife of a genius," she told me. "I did not always understand him and I felt inferior to him. He was short tempered, impatient and treated me like a cretin. Yet I still admire him. He could have taught me so much." Mildred was certainly not the scatterbrained girl that Chaplin's words would lead us to believe.

'Of his second wife, Lita Grey, another teenager, Chaplin does not even mention her name, declaring that having had two sons by her (of whom he is proud) he sees no point in giving any details about her, the marriage having been "hopeless and ending in a great deal of bitterness".

'When he met her, Chaplin was looking for a new partner. Lita Grey had played truant from school to go to the studios for a screen test. She did not get the part, but Chaplin married her instead. She was a pretty girl, laughing and charming, and of whom he does not appear to have retained very tender memories.

'He seems more generous, we must admit, towards the sparkling Paulette Goddard, whom he married, he says, during a voyage somewhere between Bali and Singapore, only to arrive at a

divorce somewhere in Mexico. When they met, Paulette was an entrancing Goldwyn show girl, and the link which attached us – writes Chaplin – was that of solitude. Paulette was shrewd, elegant, photogenic, intelligent and not prepared to be dominated. She had travelled widely, and Charlie was no longer faced with a schoolgirl. It was clear, even living with a "genius", she was going to retain her own character.

Mabel Smith, Charlie's fortune teller, predicted the happiest of futures for this couple – but for the third time happiness escaped Charlie. In the end, he was not to find it until he married his fourth wife, the charming Oona.

'Chaplin writes that it was "inevitable" that Paulette and he would separate and that they already had a presentiment of this before he started work on *The Great Dictator*. One day, Paulette packed her bags and left the Beverley Hills house, never to return.

'Chaplin is no more gallant, either, towards the wives of other men. He writes that a short time after "a marriage" of Rudolf Valentino (it can only refer to the second, since the first lasted only a few hours), his new wife deceived him with a lab boy with whom she used to disappear into the dark room.

'I knew the Italian actor and his wife very well, for I accompanied them to Europe, where we filmed some footage in 1923. And I can assure you that Rudy's romance did not last a short time but several years. Here, Charlie – who complains about gossip-mongers – does the same himself as he smugly reports what suits him about Valentino 40 years later!

'When he tells us that no man exercised a greater attraction on women than Valentino, but no man was so much deceived by them, is that not, in fact, a little piece of revenge when one remembers that the most famous Don Juan of the cinema had actually stolen Pola Negri from Charlie himself?'

THE GIFT OF LAUGHTER

Oona Chaplin, Charlie's delightful fourth wife.

Undoubtedly, the great joy of the remaining years of Charlie Chaplin's life was, as Robert Florey remarked, his marriage to Oona O'Neil, the daughter of the famous American playwright, Eugene O'Neil, and by whom he had a further eight children. Oona was just 18 years old when Charlie met her, and he was immediately captivated by her entrancing looks and strong will. Despite the disapproval of her parents, the couple were married in 1943. Oona's understanding of the man she had married, her support and her abiding love were clearly what he had sought all his life and the rest of Chaplin's life was marked by domestic harmony as one infant followed another. Oona kept very much in the background raising her family during the three decades of their marriage – much of it spent in their Swiss villa, the Manoir de Bain at Vevey, which Charlie had purchased in 1953 – and neither of them were much in the public eye. Since Charlie's death in 1977, Oona has been fiercely protective of his reputation and his work. One of the few occasions when she spoke about her husband while he was still alive occurred in 1962, when the couple were visited by the English journalist, Frederick Sands, at the time she was awaiting the birth of their last child. An interesting sidelight to her comments given below was the revelation that she called her husband, 'Charlie, my boy!', while the Chaplin children referred to their Dad rather less respectfully, but nonetheless lovingly, as 'Fatcheeks'!

Two of Charlie's children, Annette and Christopher, pictured in February 1985 with the Madame Tussaud's waxwork model of their father.

'The one inevitable subject that comes up about Charlie and myself is the difference in our ages. (He was then 72 years old, and Oona, 37). In fact, you know, I am married to a young man!

'People seem to think of Charlie as my father, but age counts for nothing in this house. To me he seems younger every day. There is certainly no father fixation about my feeling for him. He has made me mature and I keep him young.

'I never consciously think of Charlie's age for 364 days of the year. Only his birthday is the annual shock for me. But I can feel the way some people stare at me with puzzlement and then at him wondering how we have kept it up; whether it is just a facade.

'Well, my security and stability with Charlie stem not from his wealth, but from the very difference in years between us. Other young women who have married mature men will understand what I mean.

'Provided the partners are suited, such a marriage is founded on a rock, solid and with no unpleasant surprises ahead. The man's character is formed. His life is shaped. He has learned a sense of responsibility and tolerance.

'We have been blessed with children, the older ones who we keep busy and encourage to become independent. They have a place in our lives but not all of it.

'Charlie has given me one great gift that I had not known before. My childhood was not a very happy one and what he has brought to me is the gift of laughter. And *that* is beyond price.'

THE CHAPLIN LEGACY

John Doubleday's statue of Charlie which stands in Leicester Square, London – appropriately facing The Swiss Centre! An identical version also stands in Corsier sur Vevey, Switzerland, where Charlie lived during the closing years of his life.

The singer and comedian Tommy Steele who himself was born only a short distance away from Charlie's birthplace, with his unique statue of the great man.

On the eve of Charlie Chaplin's centenary, his legend is alive in the hearts of millions of men, women and children all over the world, some of whom were scarcely born when he died. It lives on not only in their imaginations, but through the showing of his movies on TV and occasionally in the cinema, but also in a constant stream of memorabilia such as books, artifacts and souvenirs (there is even an international film magazine bearing his name) as well as the memorials which have been errected to commemorate his life and work in Britain, America and Switzerland.

In London, where he was born, a six foot high bronze statue of the little tramp (actually six inches *taller* than Chaplin's real height) made by the leading sculptor, John Doubleday, stands in the heart of the city's cinemaland, Leicester Square. It was errected to mark the 92nd anniversary of his birth, and unveiled by the distinguished actor, Sir Ralph Richardson, who declared on April 16, 1981, 'I'm not unveiling a mystery – I'm unveiling a figure *everyone* knows.'

Inscribed with the words, 'The comic genius who gave pleasure to so many,' the statue was first proposed by the Greater London Council member Illtydd Harrington shortly after the star's death in 1977. It was originally to have stood at the Elephant & Castle near Charlie's birthplace, but this plan was later dropped because of lack of support from the authority concerned and because Leicester Square was felt to be a better site.

John Doubleday, a life-long admirer of Chaplin, who lives and works in Essex, based the statue on Chaplin at the peak of his popularity. He is depicted leaning on his cane, a rose pressed to his heart and – according to John – his eyes clouded with wistfulness for 'one of the girls who got away.'

John has explained that while he was working out the exact measurements for the statue he realised that Chaplin had retained all his life the underdeveloped thorax of an underfed child. But his arms and legs were 'very strong, built up by years of physically demanding work as a vaudevillian and mime.'

Curiously, about a year earlier on January 13, a statue of Charlie turned up quite unannounced in Leicester Square. The national press, intrigued by the mystery, carried stories about it the following day – only to learn that it had all been a mistake and the figure actually belonged to the famous Cockney entertainer,

Tommy Steele, himself a Chaplin admirer.

Tommy explained at the time what had happened. 'I sculpted the statue for the foyer of the Prince of Wales theatre where I have a show,' he said. 'It was cast in bronze by a firm in Scunthorpe who were due to deliver it outside the theatre. Instead they made a mistake and dumped it outside the wrong theatre, in Leicester Square!'

Tommy, of whom Fred Astaire once said, 'There's a hint of Chaplin about him', had earlier made a BBC TV programme, *In Search of Chaplin*, which was shown in April 1971, watched by 20 million people. Although he had been upset at not receiving any help from Chaplin in compiling the documentary reconstruction of his hero's life, he said, 'It was a bit puzzling, but I still discovered I was raised about 50 yards away from him in Mason Street, Southwark. Do you know, I would have loved to meet Chaplin the kid because he must have been a wonderful character.

'Of course, he's a genius, but the trouble is that his greatest enemy is the aloofness within himself in his old age. If only he were able to live in England, I'm sure he would be born again.'

Charlie has also been accorded one of the famous 'Blue Plaques' which mark the homes of famous personalities throughout Britain. His was placed on the front of 287, Kennington Road, where he lived for a time with his father and brother Sydney. It, too, was unveiled by Sir Ralph Richardson in December 1980.

Across the Atlantic in Hollywood where Charlie created his fame and fortune, there are several reminders of his presence. At 1416, North La Brea Avenue, close to the famous Sunset Boulevard, stand the row of buildings rather resembling some half-timbered English cottages, which Charlie built to serve as his studios in 1917. The studios were errected on what was then a mixture of houses, shops and vacant lots, but which is now one of the smartest streets in Hollywood.

When he was working at La Brea, Charlie was often besieged by fans and had to slip into the studios by way of the side door on De Longpre Avenue, which can still be seen today. Since 1966, the studios have belonged to A&M Records and seen the production of some best selling records and albums by leading artists.

Up in Beverley Hills, at 1085, Summit Drive, stands the Spanish-style mansion that Charlie had built in 1923, complete with tennis court and swimming pool. Stories are legion about this striking building which is hidden from view at the end of a long driveway. It is said, for instance, that Charlie used a number of his studio scenebuilders in the construction of the house, and because the men were so used to making temporary sets, parts of the structure were less than strong and actually gave way after a time! To some of Charlie's more caustic neighbours, 1085 became known as 'Breakaway House'!

Nearby, at 1143, lived two of Chaplin's closest Hollywood friends, Douglas Fairbanks and Mary Pickford, with whom, of course, he founded United Artists. Perhaps not surprisingly, this house was known as 'Pickfair'!

In 1982 Charlie's mansion was bought by film star George Hamilton and now bears his initial 'H' on the driveway gate.

A panoramic view of Charlie's Hollywood home taken not long after it was built in 1923.

In Los Angeles itself, Charlie's name is to be found on the famous 'Walk of Fame' and models of him are on display in both the Hollywood Wax Museum and the Movieland Wax Museum. In the first of these, on Hollywood Boulevard, there is a remarkably life-like statue of Charlie as the Little Tramp; while in the Movieland Wax Museum at Knott's Berry Farm near Buena Park, he is shown in a scene from *The Kid*. (Charlie in wax also appears in Madame Tussaud's in London, of course.)

Switzerland, where the little star moved with his wife in 1952 and raised his remaining eight children, has also shown pride in his residency. The Chaplin home, where Oona still lives, is an elegant villa called the Manoir de Bain, at Corsier sur Vevey, a bustling little town beside Lake Geneva. Vevey is widely known as the 'Pearl of the Swiss Riviera' and the fact that the legendary film star lived here has increased its tourist trade still further.

The Manoir, and the picturesque town with its arcaded main street and cobbled alleyways, is a lifetime away both actually and figuretively from the grimy back streets of London where Charlie was raised: a fact which no doubt came into his mind on his daily walks through the district. The area also has rich associations with writers, painters, artists and composers who settled here: Byron, Rousseau, Tallyrand and Mendelssohn are just four that spring quickly to mind.

Chaplin himself received many famous visitors at the Manoir de Bain, and local residents delight in recounting stories about these guests. One of the funniest – which perhaps understandably Charlie did *not* recount in his autobiography – concerns a dinner party and film show he gave for the Chinese Communist Premier, Chou En-lai, and a small delegation in 1954.

After the meal, the Chinese showed Charlie a film entitled, *The Ming Dynasty*, and he responded by screening *Limelight* and a trailer he had just made for *Modern Times*.

As the lights went up – the story goes – the Chinese politely enquired of Chaplin if he would be prepared to sell them the Far Eastern rights to his early silent comedies for a sum of £1,700. Never a man lost for words, Charlie turned his most charming smile on the group and said, 'What do you boys take me for – a Communist?'

Other Chaplin stories, a good many of them undoubtedly apocryphal, have helped reinforce his legend in Vevey, though some local people were less than impressed by the way he modernised his home and refer to it as 'Beverley Hills baroque'! He was, though, always welcome in Vevey, where he shopped for antique pendulum clocks, mirrors and figurines, and books in English about Napoleon, one of his favourite characters from history and who he dreamed of making a film about. 'The Three Kings' was said to be his favourite restaurant in the town.

Shortly after Charlie's funeral at Vevey on December 27, 1977, an unpleasant and rather gruesome event occurred. His body was stolen from its grave in the Corsier village cemetery by two European refugees who then attempted to extort half a million Swiss francs from Oona for its return. Thanks to some excellent police work, the two body snatchers were arrested and Charlie's body was safely recovered on March 17 from a cornfield near Lausanne where it had been hidden. It now lies once more in a theft-proof concrete tomb in the Corsier cemetery.

September 1980 saw the inauguration of the Parc Charles Chaplin in Vevey which has some uncanny similarities with the Kennington Park in London where Charlie played as a child. Indeed, one section of it mirrors very closely West Square where the boy lived for a short time.

In the Parc stands a bronze replica of the statue of Chaplin that John Doubleday created for London. It was errected in August 1982 and has since become a focal point for many visitors. Also drawing ever-increasing audiences is the Annual Film Festival of Comedy held in memory of Charlie, and of which Oona is the honorary president. The premier awards at the festival are, predictably, golden walking sticks which the Swiss refer to as 'Canes'!

Since Chaplin's death there has been a great deal of rumour and speculation about 'lost' works by the master. He was known to have been working on at least two film ideas in the years preceding his death.

The most advanced of these projects was a story called *The Freak* about an angel who comes down to earth, and changes the lives of all those she meets. Charlie wrote the screenplay with his daughter, Victoria, in mind as the angel. He also wanted to star another member of his family, his son Sydney, then in his fifties, in a second movie about a prisoner on death row who escapes and finds it is like being born again.

Earlier in his lifetime, Charlie had many other ideas for pictures – perhaps the most intriguing of these being *The Moon Olympics* which he outlined in 1916! This movie, which would surely have

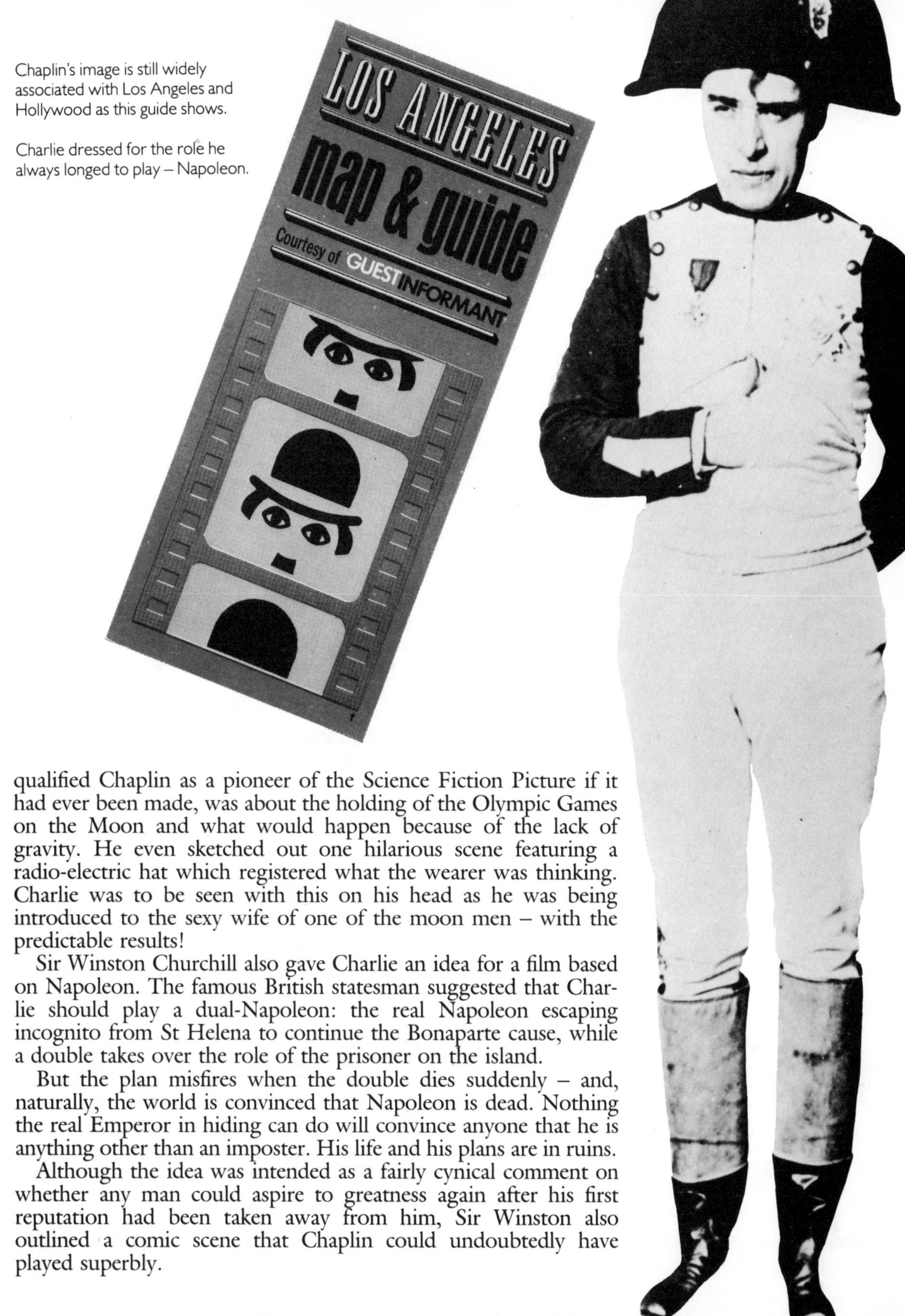

Chaplin's image is still widely associated with Los Angeles and Hollywood as this guide shows.

Charlie dressed for the role he always longed to play – Napoleon.

qualified Chaplin as a pioneer of the Science Fiction Picture if it had ever been made, was about the holding of the Olympic Games on the Moon and what would happen because of the lack of gravity. He even sketched out one hilarious scene featuring a radio-electric hat which registered what the wearer was thinking. Charlie was to be seen with this on his head as he was being introduced to the sexy wife of one of the moon men – with the predictable results!

Sir Winston Churchill also gave Charlie an idea for a film based on Napoleon. The famous British statesman suggested that Charlie should play a dual-Napoleon: the real Napoleon escaping incognito from St Helena to continue the Bonaparte cause, while a double takes over the role of the prisoner on the island.

But the plan misfires when the double dies suddenly – and, naturally, the world is convinced that Napoleon is dead. Nothing the real Emperor in hiding can do will convince anyone that he is anything other than an imposter. His life and his plans are in ruins.

Although the idea was intended as a fairly cynical comment on whether any man could aspire to greatness again after his first reputation had been taken away from him, Sir Winston also outlined a comic scene that Chaplin could undoubtedly have played superbly.

Napoleon, at the height of his fame, was to be seen lying pot-bellied and naked in his bath. His lieutenants would then choose this moment to burst in upon him, believing him to be at a disadvantage without his splendid uniform. But as they put their demands to him, Napoleon begins to splash them. Dampened, they retreat a little. The Emperor then splashes more violently – and the men are soaked. As they retire demoralised, the point is made that greatness can still triumph – even in the bath!

There have been a number of instances of so-called 'undiscovered' Chaplin films coming to light. For some years, intensive searches were being made in America for two pictures entitled *Charlie Chaplin in a Harem* and *Charlie Chaplin, Son of the Gods*. Unlikely though both sounded, they were eventually traced – both of them being fakes that had been made by the Apollo Film Corporation in Los Angeles in 1917.

As recently as September 1985, it was reported that two dozen unknown Chaplin short movies had been found during excavation of a building site in Hollywood where a new restaurant was being constructed. Some of these pictures were even said to contain 'experimental sound tracks'. Although the 'find' quickly made TV and press headlines, Chaplin experts were immediately suspicious about such a cache because 24 films would represent something like two years of the star's output and no such period of his career was unaccounted for. The suspicion was well-founded: for the pictures proved to be just a batch of Chaplin two-reelers reissued in the 1930's with inferior sound-tracks. But the media attention which the discovery attracted demonstrated once again the magic of the Chaplin name.

The most important and genuine 'finds' of recent years were two substantially complete pictures, *How To Make Movies* and *The Professor*, plus many thousands of feet of rushes and deleted sequences from Chaplin pictures, unearthed by two British researchers, David Gill and Kevin Brownlow.

These men had come across the first signs of these dazzling prizes while researching a TV series, *Hollywood*, for Thames TV in the mid-1970s.

It was not until several years later, however, after Charlie's death, that Gill and Brownlow were able to begin work on a documentary series in which they hoped to utilise the long-hidden material. Kevin Brownlow has described what happened when they began to view the reels of celluloid in the Chaplin vaults:

'We found ourselves watching superlative quality prints of Chaplin footage never before seen in public. A complete, edited sequence from *City Lights* (as simple and brilliant as anything Chaplin ever did), a scene from *Modern Times*, rushes from three unused sequences for *The Circus*, and fragments for a film about his studio. We were soon reeling with the impact of it all . . .

'When we approached Oona Chaplin, she agreed it would be wrong to suppress what were in effect the working notes of one of the greatest film-makers of our time. Her permission gave us access, in the preparation of our programmes, to use out-takes, abandoned projects, rushes, shots of Chaplin at work, his studio,

The complete Little Tramp's outfit – three items of which, the hat, cane and shoes fetched the astronomical sum of £121,000 at a London auction in December 1987!

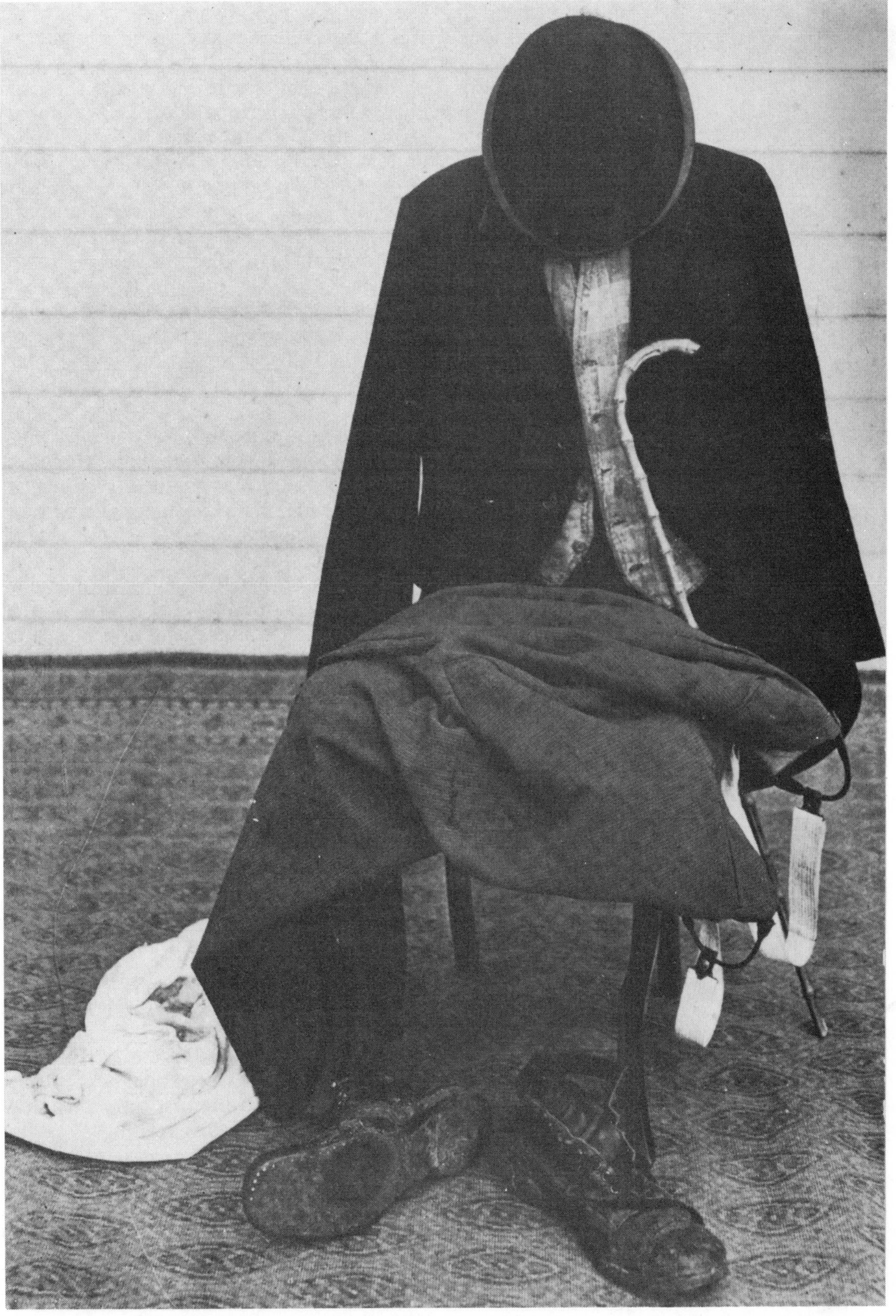

and sequences that were cut from his famous films – it was the equivalent of finding long-lost sketchbooks of Rembrandt.'

The result of these researches was a three-part series, *The Unknown Chaplin*, broadcast in January 1983, which at last made public the two previously unseen pictures. *How To Make Movies*, as it's title suggests, is a comedy documentary about Chaplin at work in his studios, and had been made in 1918. *The Professor*, on the other hand, was pure invention, featuring a Flea Circus owner, Professor Bosco, played by Chaplin, which the maestro had shot a year later but never released. (Chaplin did, though, utilise some of the gags from this picture in *Limelight*.)

The Unknown Chaplin had a tremendous impact on both film experts and the general public. 'For three hours,' Chaplin expert David Robinson summed-up on behalf of the entire viewing population, 'we were privileged to see the greatest comic mind at work.' (Surprisingly, though, to date this series has not been shown in the USA!)

Although it is unlikely that any more new film by Chaplin will emerge (I hesitate to include still photography, as rumours abound concerning caches of jealously guarded pictures), the demand for Chapliana continues at a furious pace. In particular, the souvenirs and artifacts from his working life are now fetching almost astronomical sums at auction.

In December 1987, for instance, a sale of Chaplin mementoes at Christie's in London fetched a total of £157,609, of which £121,000 was paid for just three items of his tramp's gear – the hat, cane and shoes! A Swiss museum bid £38,000 for the boots, and Mr Jorgen Strecker, the owner of a Danish entertainment centre paid a combined figure of £82,500 for the hat and cane. These two items had been estimated at £10,000 to £15,000 each!

All three items were authenticated with the stamp, 'Chaplin Studios Inc' and an accompanying letter explained that the cane had been especially preserved by Chaplin's manager, Alfred Reeves because 'Charlie liked it and used it constantly.' The boots were described as having 'distressed leather soles, the heel of the right boot containing a hole for stunt work'. Apparently, throughout his entire career Charlie had only used three pairs of boots – one pair were deemed to be uncomfortable and rejected, and the third were eaten by mice!

On the tenth anniversary of Chaplin's death, Christie's also held an auction of memorabilia which again underlined just how widely Charlie's image had been utilised and what a craze there must have been for such merchandising. Indeed, it was claimed that Chaplin had been the first show business personality to inspire a whole industry in souvenirs. It was also the first time a whole sale had been devoted to commemorative items relating to a single personality!

Among the more than 250 items seen at the sale were fairly predictable items such as Chaplin toys, games and statuettes in every kind of material and size, as well as some more surprising *objets d'art* like jewellery, car mascots, bottles, pudding moulds, table lamps, musical boxes, bottlestoppers, salt cellars, tobacco jars, umbrellas, money boxes, wristwatches and walking sticks!

In writing about the auction, Janet Marsh of the *Financial Times* found herself absolutely amazed at this vast array of mementoes of the little tramp whom she referred to as 'perhaps the most universally recognised figure in film history.' I doubt that she needed to qualify that statement with the word 'perhaps'. For *who* is there to rival Chaplin as we mark his centenary?

And perhaps one might even ask further: is there *ever* likely to be anyone to rival his unique and remarkable achievement?

Boxford, Suffolk
June, 1988

A youthful Charlie with a Chaplin doll – one of the first of what became a flood of merchandising items which are now much sought after by collectors.

ACKNOWLEDGEMENTS

The majority of people who helped me in the writing of this book are acknowledged in the text, but I should also just like to record my special thanks to W.O.G. Lofts for his invaluable help with the research and Mrs Pamela Chamberlaine for her translation work. I am also grateful to the following for supplying photographs and other illustrated material used in the book: the British Film Institute, The American Film Institute, Universal Pictures, United Artists, Solo Picture Agency, Keystone Press and The Picture Source. These newspapers and magazines have also allowed me to quote from their pages: *The Times, The Observer, Daily Telegraph, Evening Standard, Sunday Mirror, Sunday Times, Daily Mail, Sunday Express, The People, The Morning Star, Punch, Radio Times, Cinemonde, Films & Filming, The Ciné-Technician, Variety, Photoplay,* and *Sight & Sound.* As always, I am indebted to my friends at the British Film Institute in London for their help and suggestions in the writing of this tribute to 'The Little Tramp'.